CHANGE YOUR DAY, NOT YOUR LIFE

CHANGE YOUR DAY, NOT YOUR LIFE

A REALISTIC GUIDE TO SUSTAINED MOTIVATION, MORE PRODUCTIVITY, AND THE ART OF WORKING WELL

ANDY CORE

WILEY

To my wife, Naomi Core,
and my little girls, Bella and Camille:
I cannot thank you enough for your love,
support, and for showing me
what truly matters.

And also to my mom: Everything good in me is
because of you.

My brothers, Matt and Jess Core:
Team Core.

My mentor and friend, David Pincus,
whose vast intellect is only matched by the
size of his heart.

Jan Dargatz, a true master in the art of
writing and communication.

To my clients, who have trusted me to
share in their journey.

Contents

Preface

The sheer amount of work you do each day can leave you tired, stressed, and less than enchanted with work and life. The problem and the paradox are this: hardworking adults striving to grow often end up defaulting to a daily life that is undermining their ability to succeed. Have you experienced the symptoms of this paradox?

- No energy
- Distracted and unconnected
- Too busy to be productive
- Too worried to be fully present today

Author Andy Core can help you beat this. For over two decades, Andy has helped working adults and organizations all over the United States, Asia, and Europe add positive energy to their work, teams, and personal lives. And he does so with a surprisingly simple premise—Change Your Day, Not Your Life.

You will better understand "Why am I so tired?" "Why am I so stressed?" "Why don't I want to do what I know I should do?"

You will learn to beat "Motivational Amnesia," the strange phenomenon in which your motivation to hit your goals can be high one day, but disappear the next . . . then reappear . . . and on and on . . .

You will learn specific mini-patterns that you can plug into your day that will trigger the best parts of who you are to emerge or brighten and become more powerful drivers of what you do and how you think.

Change Your Day will introduce you to "Thrivers, Strivers, and Strugglers," and ask the question, "What makes some people thrive in high-demand environments while others struggle?" The answers are simple. Thrivers:

- Are better at how they mentally approach their work, especially under pressure.
- Are better at keeping their energy up.
- Are more clear about why they are working so hard.
- Are better at designing the flow of their day.

Next, you identify where you stand with these Core characteristics. Then, you will learn specific examples of how Thrivers use these ideas in the real world.

And finally, it will help you Change Your Day, but not your whole day. You will start building mini-patterns into your day that will become part of your way of life and will consistently fuel your motivation, productivity, and ability to work and live well.

With this book you will turn wasted hours into tasks accomplished. You will find you want to live healthier, even though that was not your intention. It will fuel your want to achieve great things, just for the sake of achievement. In the end, you will create sustainable motivation, be more productive, and will be able to work and live well.

CHAPTER 1

A Secret behind the Magic

A hired car glided smoothly into the pick-up area in front of the MBA advertising agency in London. Two advertising agency executives climbed into the car at the chauffer's directive. They had no idea where they were going or why. They at least knew they weren't being kidnapped—they were only going on a secret assignment.

The executives settled into the backseat and watched the buildings go by as they were driven through the heart of London. They soon arrived at a business office, where they were greeted by Darren Brown, a well-known illusionist in the United States and the United Kingdom, and the host of a popular television show titled *Mind Control*.

As they sat down in a conference room at Brown's direction, they were given this challenge: "Design a logo and strap line (slogan) for a new chain of stores." The product? Taxidermy, the stuffing and preserving of dead animals.

Before he allowed the advertising executives to begin their design work, Brown announced he had already drawn up some ideas and had put them in a sealed envelope, which he had placed under a stuffed cat on the conference room table. Brown gave them 30 minutes to complete their task, and he left the room.

The ad men immediately launched into full brainstorming mode. They identified various ideas and themes, threw out most of them as "ridiculous," and then focused on one idea and developed it as best they could in the time given.

Brown returned to the room and the men revealed their ideas:

- **Logo:** A bear sitting on a cloud playing a harp.
- **Slogan:** "Animal Heaven: The best place for the best dead animals."

Brown complimented them on their creativity and then asked them to open the sealed envelope he had left in the room. They opened the envelope and as they read the contents, the blood seemed to drain from both of their faces. One of the men dropped his head into his hands as he thought, *I've been gutted.*

Brown's document showed:

- The sketch of a logo with a bear sitting on a cloud playing a harp.
- The slogan assigned to the logo read, "Creature Heaven: Where the best dead animals go."

The wording was not identical, but it was close enough to be uncanny.

How did Darren Brown influence these two highly paid creative professionals—whose livelihood was to come up with original ideas—to draw nearly the same logo and write nearly the same slogan that he had developed?

Was there a secret?

Yes.

As the ad men walked out of the building to get back into the car Brown had sent, their attention was caught by a painting on the wall of a nearby building—plainly in their line of sight as they had arrived at Brown's office. It was a painting of a bear. As they reviewed the route to the meeting, they noted that they had first been driven past the London Zoo. At a stoplight by the zoo, a group of people walked across the crosswalk: All were wearing light blue sweatshirts with the word "Zoo" printed across the front. At the next stoplight, to their right, they had seen a department store window with a big harp on display. They were then driven past a coffee shop with a chalkboard outside that included the words, "Creature Heaven." As they had entered Brown's building, they had walked past a man holding a flip chart with more subtle cues.

In the time that it took to drive these two ad men across town, Darren Brown had cued . . . influenced . . . triggered . . . and motivated these men to think and act in a very specific way.

Scary, huh?

When I first read about this incident, I was so fascinated by it that I decided to test it on several audiences, with a combined total of 9,000 people. One of the audiences had 4,000 health-care designers, creative people by training and experience. I asked these audience members to do the same exercise Brown had prescribed: draw a logo and invent a slogan for a series of taxidermy shops. I did not, however, give them any of the "cues" that Brown had known were along the ad men's drive to his office.

Without the cues the ad men were exposed to on their trip in London, how many in my audience do you think drew a logo with a bear—much less a bear sitting on a cloud playing a harp? You're right if you said *none*.

Of the 9,000 people asked to come up with a slogan, how many of them used the phrase "Animal Heaven" or "Creature Heaven"? You're right if you said *zero*.

There has been an active debate through the years as to whether "subliminal" advertising works—most experts agree that it does *not* work. Hidden messages don't seem to have much of a mysterious influence on us. But, at the same time, research has shown consistently that cues have a surprising effect on us. Environmental triggers—those things we encounter and perceive as we go through our lives, whether they are consciously or unconsciously perceived—*do* influence our attitudes, thoughts, emotions, and behaviors—far more so than most might think.

HAVE YOU EVER ASKED . . .

Have you ever asked yourself, "Why don't I *want* to do what I know I should do?"

Have you ever thought, "Why don't I seem to be as happy as I should be, given what is going on in my life?"

Have you ever questioned, "Why am I more cranky or tired or less patient than I should be, given the facts of my life?"

The truth is, your day is a series of cues that trigger how you feel, act, and think much more than you may realize.

From the moment you awaken, the supercomputer between your ears begins to take in a wide variety of information through all of your senses. These cues trigger a sequence of thoughts, feelings, and actions that build upon one another—each thought, feeling, or act becomes another cue.

The momentum associated with these cues builds not only in the moment, but throughout the day. Each passing hour adds more cues, forming the "conclusions" about your day—it is a good day or a bad day, you are feeling positive or negative, you have been productive or unproductive, you are energized or you are drained, and so forth.

That prevailing opinion of your day likely carries on into your sleep, and determines an "upon awakening" set of cues that begin your next day.

Over time, the cues you routinely take into your mind can create a prevailing attitudinal "world view"—one in which you can eventually feel trapped without even knowing that you have been taken captive. Cues can eventually produce a general attitude—pessimism, optimism, fatalism, or any of a number of other "isms."

Perhaps the most insidious of all facts related to this is: What you imagine—or the series of thoughts that play out in your mind—are cues that trigger you. You will begin to look for, validate, and reinforce the cues that you think about, even if you have not encountered those cues in real life.

Let me give you an example: Close your eyes and imagine that you are walking down a sidewalk past a small bakery. The aroma of cinnamon and yeast bread is filling the air. You can almost feel yourself salivate at the idea.

Does this smell trigger you to quicken your pace to "out-walk" the temptation? Do you veer into the bakery and lay claim to one of the biggest and most sumptuous cinnamon rolls you have ever seen?

In the aftermath, do you feel proud of yourself for resisting? Guilty for succumbing? What do those thoughts trigger? Will it trigger a change in your lunch plans? Will it impact your communication with people you now perceive as cinnamon-roll-worthy colleagues, or those you believe should abstain from having as many cinnamon rolls as they seem to be eating?

These cues and triggers build upon one another and become basic patterns of thinking and feeling!

To Change Your Day . . .

To change your day, begin by considering the cues that you encounter on a daily basis.

If the cues you are experiencing are not serving you well—if you don't like the way you are thinking, feeling, or acting—make an intentional decision to refocus your attention, to redirect your imagination and patterns of thinking, and to begin to absorb cues that you believe can create greater motivation, energy, productivity, optimism, creativity, and more rewarding relationships with others.

People who thrive in a high-demand world:

- Take a more intentional approach to what they PERCEIVE.

- Choose to really look at their world, and be aware of what is being absorbed into their conscious and subconscious minds.

- Build their daily life so that it consistently cues greater and greater positive energy.

CHAPTER 2

Behavioral Momentum

The CEO of a Fortune 100 company stood on the stage, behind a lectern and in front of a large digital display panel. On the display were the words "Thank You!" along with the logo of their "Platinum Award."

The event was part of an incentive trip for the top salespeople in the corporation, and it was being held on the island of St. Martin in the Caribbean. Only the top 1 percent of salespeople had been invited. The audience of several hundred people was attending this very special corporate meeting. They looked very festive in their Hawaiian-print shirts, swimsuit cover-ups, and flip-flops.

The CEO said, "As you know, this trip is not about work, but reward. Today we officially announce the top 10 sales reps of our entire company."

As the CEO then announced the reps, one by one, he began with number 10 and counted his way down, generally adding a comment that went something like this: "Ben Smith, of the Southeast region, who has the account with Company ABC, which grew X percent over last year to a total of X thousands of dollars."

This general statement accompanied the introduction of the reps numbers 10 to 5. When the CEO reached the rep in position number 4, he said: "Barry Ozturk, from the South Central region, whose account with ABC . . ." and then he flipped over the page in front of him to keep reading, "DEF, GHI, JKL Companies . . ." He paused and with amazement in his voice, he continued, "Wow, Barry produced X percentage increase this year and did so without a primary account."

Most reps who reach the Platinum-Award level in this company have only one big account. Barry had reached the number 4 spot by hustling among several small and medium-sized accounts, which is significantly harder and very rare.

I had made a presentation to this conference right before this awards event and was listening to the CEO from backstage. After I heard the presentation, I tracked down Barry and arranged to have breakfast with him the next morning. My main question to Barry was, "How did you do it?"

He said, "Andy, by nine o'clock every morning, most of my peers are sitting at their desks finishing their read of the morning paper. By nine o'clock, I've already met with two to three new prospects. I've exercised, eaten a healthy breakfast, and had coffee with my wife."

He continued, "I'm not trying to say that my coworkers are lazy. They are not. I know many are working past eight o'clock on most worknights. I just don't think that is the most productive way to live, and it is certainly not the way I choose to live."

I could see how such a fixed routine might work for a person who goes into a main office every day, but that was not the case with Barry. He told me, "My days are always different. Some are in the office. Sometimes I am traveling or meeting with people. Other days are spent doing paperwork. But, I have very consistent patterns."

Barry's pattern goes like this: He wakes up early, walks to the opposite side of the room to the table where his alarm clock sits. He flips the alarm off—no snoozing. He walks into his closet and puts on exercise clothes that he has laid out the night before. He goes immediately to the gym, the treadmill in his home, or jogs outside for 30 minutes. He cools off after his exercise, has a mug of coffee from his programmable coffee maker (which was preset the night before), and sits down to eat a breakfast that he also laid out the night before. He eats while reading the newspaper or a business journal. He showers, spends a few minutes with his wife and children, and then heads out the door.

His first two meetings or activities were scheduled the day before. After those meetings, he usually swings by the home office—about midmorning—and checks messages or attends meetings that set in motion appointments for the remainder of his day.

Barry's patterns are highly predictable, and over the months and now years, those patterns have had measurable results in his life. His patterns have produced progress that he can feel and see—and much of that progress happens even before his peers have finished reading the morning paper.

I can hear some of you thinking, "Yeah, Andy. Barry is a go-getter." That's only one point to be gleaned from his life. The *greater* point is this—Barry's first-things-first approach to a day sets in motion a pattern that *continues* throughout his day. The positive momentum he creates early in his day cues a productive rest of the day. The truth is this: What you do *first* matters.

Core Concept: What you do *first* matters.

Sir Isaac Newton once said, "Objects in motion tend to stay in motion."

From my perspective and after countless conversations with "go-getters," I firmly believe that the ideas, actions, thoughts, and feelings that a person sets in motion first thing in the morning tend to not only stay in motion, they have a great likelihood of gaining in momentum throughout a day, especially if those ideas, actions, thoughts, and feelings occur in a rapid sequence.

There Is a Better Way to Start the Day

By the time Barry got to his office, he had already ticked off several important boxes on his list of things to do, and he was geared toward continuing that pace for the next several hours—while his peers were still in the starting blocks looking for their first box to check off!

WHAT BEHAVIORAL MOMENTUM ACCOMPLISHES

Behavioral Momentum is a well-documented theory in the realm of motivation, and it is a key means of increasing "compliance" or "stick-to-it-iveness" in goal setting.

The theory proposes that if you want someone to do a fairly difficult activity, which that person may not initially want to do, then ask the person to do one or two fairly easy activities before you ask him to do the more difficult activity. The person's success—perhaps even enjoyment at the task or the enjoyment at having accomplished the task—sets up the person to want to continue the success, and to give greater positive effort to accomplishing the difficult task.

Core Concept: Motivation is really momentum in disguise.

In Barry's case, day after day of successful productivity had a similar momentum effect. Days of high productivity set Barry up for weeks of high productivity, until this pattern became a predictable habit that continually, consistently motivated him to his best behavior with the most positive attitude and most creative ideas. The clients with whom he met, of course, were encountering an upbeat, creative, energized rep—and his overall positive "performance" in their presence encouraged them to buy, and then buy some more!

Behavioral Momentum produces a formula of:

$$1 + 1 + 1 = 10$$

Momentum is a multiplication process. It produces a geometric curve.

I have met dozens of people who tell me that when they began to see real progress toward a new goal they had set for themselves, they began to feel the impact of momentum. They began to think, *This makes me feel great! I can do this! Why wasn't I doing it before?* The initial success is both reinforcing and motivating.

But what happens if a person gives up, or falls out of the new routine? The reverse kicks in. It doesn't take long before a person loses consistency, motivation wanes, and goals fade. Before long the person is thinking, *How was I ever able to do that?*

THINGS CAN BE TURNED AROUND

Have you ever left a sporting event before the end of the game or competition because one team was getting hammered so badly that the game had become boring? And then, on the drive home, as you turned on the radio to get the final score of what you just knew was a wipe-out, you hear that the losing team is staging an amazing comeback, and one that eventually produces a squeak-by victory in the last seconds?

How could momentum change so quickly?

Have you ever arrived at work feeling energized, positive, focused, and highly motivated—and then reflected later in the day on how rewarding those first few tasks or appointments of your day turned out to be? But then, the next day, you came to work after a rough, perhaps sleepless night, bad traffic problems, angry words with your significant other, and you glare at those in your office, thinking, *All these happy people are getting on my nerves!*

What makes the difference?

Have you ever wondered how just one negative performance can change your attitude so quickly—and conversely, how one major "score" can create many more positive vibes and even a few more social invitations than you ever thought possible?

Why are people so fickle?

Have you ever wondered how you can feel incredibly cranky toward your child or significant other in one moment, and at the same time feel deep love for that person?

The answer to all of the questions above is this: DO-KNOW-BE.

Core Concept: DO-KNOW-BE

Break it down.

    DO

    KNOW

    BE

What you DO usually *starts* a cycle that triggers a deeper understanding of what you KNOW (information, ideas, attitudes, feelings), which results in a state of *being* (your character).

This is counter to what many people believe.

They think that a person has a character that is intact, and out of this, a person learns facts or produces ideas and feelings, and this "knowledge" base motivates the person's behavior.

This belief, that if you know something is important and worthwhile, then you should want to do it, is one of the primary drivers of the ultimately frustrating question, "Why don't I do what I know I should?" Study after study in behavior change show that the opposite is true. Get somebody to DO something, and out of their doing, they will develop attitudes, ideas, and feelings. If what they do is successful and positive, they will learn that this DOing is good! It is beneficial, rewarding, and pleasurable. They will want to do it again . . . and again. If the behavior is healthful, positive, and rewarding, the information (ideas and feelings and attitudes) they gain will compel them to create a new habit of doing, and over time, it is our habits of behavior combined with our habits of thinking/feeling that produce our character.

Larry Winget, the Pitbull of Personal Development™, says, "Nothing in life gets better until you do." I agree, and think of it like this, "Nothing in your life gets better until your daily patterns do. But, when your daily patterns get better, everything gets better."

SHIFT OUT OF A KNOW-BE-DO PATTERN

There are a number of organizations, and even entire industries that have bought into a KNOW-DO-BE pattern. They believe that if they can just get enough of the right information, benefits, or commands to their people, they will see behavioral changes.

The messages issued are often relentless and even obnoxious.

The messages are generally geared to telling others all of the nasty things that will happen if the rules are broken, the process fails, the goals are not met. And conversely, messages are given that tell all of the wonderful things that may happen if the messages are heeded.

We need to get real about this.

The truth is that the vast majority of people KNOW that continual absenteeism is going to result in workplace discipline and perhaps the loss of a job. The vast majority of people in our culture KNOW that smoking is bad for you, that you should buckle your seatbelt, that drugs are bad for a teenager, and that obesity can have all sorts of health consequences, none of them good.

Awareness campaigns are only effective if the people being given the messages are *unaware*.

Let me be very practical in giving an example.

Let's say that your company wants its employees—including you—to have your blood drawn and tested once a year to ensure you stay healthy.

Telling you that you should get your blood tested is helpful, but not the most effective thing to do. It is far more effective if a mobile blood testing van is invited to pull into the parking lot outside your office. And what is even more effective is a supervisor who asks you, "*When* do you want to take off to go get your blood tested . . . let's schedule it right now on my calendar so I know when you will be away—just like we schedule vacation time."

Such a supervisor is not approaching you from a KNOW perspective, but from a behavioral DO perspective. Making the appointment and going to the appointment are behavioral acts, not mental exercises.

Overall, changing what you think—also known as "adjusting your attitude" or "expanding your information base"—does not always result in action.

Action, however, DOES always change the way you think!

Kelly McGonigal, a psychologist and Stanford professor and author of a book titled *The Willpower Instinct*, stated that it is generally futile to try to fix our thinking by clearing up anxiety or fears before we take an active step toward doing something. Rather, we are better off to launch out and take action—in spite of and often in the face of our fears or past failures. When we lead with DO, our experience actually modifies our perspective and very often changes our level of anxiety or fear. In the DOing, we gain valuable information that is motivating. We learn more about ourselves, more about how to reach our goals, and more about HOW to act in ways that are increasingly beneficial and positive. Motivation is more of an *experiential* lesson than an *informational* one.

I'm all for being a DO-KNOW-BE!

One of my favorite sales trainers is Terri Sjodin, and one of my favorite quotes she has made is this: "Be a closer, not a concluder." If you want someone to do something, don't end your message to that person with the statement, "In conclusion, I want you to think long and hard about this." Rather, end your appointment with, "Here's my pen . . . are you ready to sign on?" Instead of, "You should get your blood tested," a more effective approach is, "Our wellness team has set up a blood testing station in this room and at these times. What time can you go?"

> ## Core Concept: When you want people to do something, direction beats information seven days a week.

NO MATTER THE TERRITORY

I believe it is also important to tell you that Barry's territory was one of the worst that the company had. Barry didn't succeed because he was working highly fertile, rich sales fields. He was succeeding in spite of poor soil.

His success was not only because of his ability to build Behavioral Momentum.

Barry is a Thriver.

To Change Your Day . . .

- Remember, "Nothing in your life gets better until your daily patterns do. But, when your daily patterns get better, everything gets better."

- Be a DO-KNOW-BE: Lasting motivation is an experiential lesson.

- Take time to reflect on the way your daily behaviors produce attitudes, feelings, and ideas.

- Consider how you can proactively design your daily life so that you are fueling the person you want to be.

CHAPTER 3

Hope Like a Thriver

Everybody I know, including myself, can come up with dozens of excuses—some of them legitimate and some of them very creative—to explain why they *don't* do the things they want to do. There are many reasons for a failure in a job or relationship that lie beyond the effort or quantity and quality of time that a person gives to a task or goal.

Rather than focus on *why* failure might occur, I encourage you to ask, "What do the high-achieving, fulfilled, purposeful, and happy people do?"

In my experience, most working adults put in good effort. They don't have major character flaws or personality disorders. They don't lack values. Even so, they tell me with a fair degree of regularity that they feel:

- Too tired to reenergize themselves.
- Too distracted to feel "connected" to others.
- Too busy to accomplish the things that are most meaningful to them.
- Too worried about the future to be fully present "in the moment."

What are *these* people to do?
And why is change so difficult?

THE RENEWING POWER OF HOPE

After researching working adults for over two decades, from the United States to Asia and Europe, I have discovered that nearly all people in high-demand jobs or stages of life fit into one of three general categories: Thrivers, Strivers, and Strugglers.

- **Strugglers** are those who are not fit for high-demand workplaces. They either don't want to or are not ready to *work hard*. They nearly always leave or are "liberated" by an organization to pursue what they perceive to be greener pastures requiring less grazing effort. While it is possible to motivate or give new perspective to Strugglers, they are not the focus of this book. They are a study unto themselves.

- **Strivers** are those who work hard, often meet their own expectations and those of their superiors at work, but often struggle with high levels of stress and of *maintaining* a high quality of work, life, and attitude. They want to succeed in all areas of their life, but may not have the skills or a plan about *how* to succeed.

- **Thrivers** are those who work hard, consistently meet or exceed their expectations at work, and who experience high levels of success with only low levels of stress both professionally and personally.

Let me add here that I do not believe it is possible to live an entirely stress-free life, in part because a certain amount of stress is necessary *for* growth, high performance, and high achievement. Ask even the most experienced performer, athlete, or business mogul about whether he ever feels a little tension as he prepares to walk on stage, take on a competitor, or finalize a deal. He will nearly always will say, "yes." Thrivers, however, have mastered the mental skills to release that pre-performance stress and to limit its impact apart from the precise time frame of their performance, competition, or high-impact meeting.

There are a number of other very specific characteristics and behaviors associated with each of these three categories, but in this chapter, I want to address only one characteristic associated with Thrivers.

First, let's consider Barry, whom we met in the previous chapter. He was a Thriver. He wasn't just working (striving), he was achieving. He rarely asked the question "Why don't I do what I know I should?" He wasn't just dreaming of rewards, he was earning them, receiving them, and enjoying them. He was not only successful in one area of his life. His entire life had the earmarks of success.

Barry's attitude and way of life helped him eliminate any "Motivational Amnesia." That is my term for the phenomenon in which a person's motivation can be high one day and disappear the next, only to reappear, for sometimes no apparent reason. Values, genetics, and personal history don't change, but a person nevertheless seems to lose motivation, even forget who they are, what they are capable of doing, or why they *want* to be at their peak in both performance and character day in and day out.

Barry was able to sustain a fairly even—and highly enviable—flow of Behavioral Momentum, without bouts of Motivational Amnesia. This was one of the traits that made him a bona fide Thriver.

At the core of Thriving is *hope*.

It sounds simple . . . and it is. But hope is often a very difficult thing to conjure up and sustain. Barry had developed a way of life that built his confidence that he would be successful at work and in his personal life, and this provides a fertile ground for hope to grow.

Some time ago, I sat in a large auditorium, listening to a presentation from one of the leading behavior-change experts of our time. He was making me lose hope. He cited highly negative trends:

- The United States is becoming more and more obese every year, and the result is that morbid obesity (the level of obesity that has deadly consequence) is at near-epidemic levels.
- Up to 75 percent of workers in the United States are not fully engaged in their work, and do not feel motivated to improve their work output, workplace morale, or levels

of efficiency; job satisfaction is near an all-time low across many industries and professions.

- Divorce rates are still very high, and rising.
- Credit-card debt is at an all-time high.

And on and on he went.

He told of a statistic related to heart attacks that I found especially troubling. It seems that physicians routinely tell those who have survived serious heart attacks that they can significantly lower their chance of having another heart attack if they will begin to live in a healthier way—specifically, to exercise, eat more fiber, lose weight if they are overweight, give up smoking, and take the medications prescribed for their heart health with regularity.

One major study found that six out of seven patients who heard this advice from their cardiologists did not start—or did not sustain—the healthier life prescribed for them. A high percentage didn't even fill the prescriptions given to them, much less take those medications with regularity. The presenter then stated, "Physicians know that a person has a much better chance of being cured of cancer than of permanently losing weight."

My heart sank. I thought, *If people won't change, even when their life is on the line, what chance do we have of getting them to improve things that are not directly life-threatening?*

A friend told me about a young child who had heard some bad news and responded with a clever phrase to the bad-news bearer: "You are cranking me down." This guy was seriously cranking me down!

And then a thought, and a bit of anger, kicked in. *Hey, wait a minute. I know a great many people who are changing and who have changed, even when change seemed nearly impossible. I've personally helped many people to change—to*

*become more productive, less stressed, and healthier. And fur-
thermore, I've seen these people sustain positive changes.*

I walked out of that presentation with a firm conclusion:
Yes, it may be disheartening, even depressing, that six of seven
people don't change or fail in their attempts to change—even
when their life is in balance. But . . . that means there is one
of every seven who does change—even in the aftermath of a
serious heart attack. There is one in every seven who manages
to change and sustain change.

SEEK OUT THE ONE IN SEVEN

Human nature seems to drive us to focus on the six out of
seven people who fail to change or sustain change. Thrivers
are those who overcome this tendency and choose to focus on
the one in seven who do change. They tend to focus more on
the one in seven in their personal actions.

Focusing on the one in seven who do change . . . who
do grow . . . who do overcome their motivational amnesia . . . who do begin again and build momentum . . . are
people who have greater hope. Focus on the positive one
in seven in your own life. And hope is like the "additive"
that gives higher octane to a person's performance. Hope
is what helps a person DO even in the face of difficulty.
And remember, it is what a person DOES that is the primary kick-starter to having more of everything good in life,
including powerful, sustained motivation.

It seems to be human nature to love the underdog in just
about any arena of competition. In the area of motivation, I
call the "one in seven" the Change Underdogs. I encourage
you to seek out those who are succeeding in spite of *everything* life has thrown at them. It is only when you seek out the
one in seven that you will find them—the six out of seven are

a lot more visible and a lot more entrenched in their resistance to all things that are positive and encouraging.

Look specifically for people who are doing what you want to achieve. Use them as your role models. The nine most motivating words you can say are, *"If they could do it, I can do it."*

A 2005 study published in the *American Journal of Ophthalmology* was done with people who suffer from glaucoma. They each were given a prescription for eye drops to help their condition. The downside was that they had to use these eye drops up to 10 times a day. The upside was a high probability that they could retain their eyesight.

Within six months, half of the people had stopped taking their eye drops, and the result was that their glaucoma worsened. In three years, barely a third were even fulfilling the prescription for the eye drops. They had lost hope in their ability to change. They no longer had hope of retaining their eyesight over the next few years. They had allowed discouragement to overcome hope.

It happens more than we like to admit. And sometimes it doesn't take much to push a person into doubt, anxiety and worry, discouragement, and depression.

We each must become the foremost person to proclaim to ourselves:

I will stay focused on *hope*!

Those who focus on the six people out of seven not only suffer from failure, but they suffer in their emotions and attitudes and often fall into despair.

Those who see the one person in seven are Thrivers. They are hopeful. They refuse to give up on hope. They refuse to cave in to periodic loss or downturns. They keep focused on what can still be good, and they surround themselves as much as possible with people who are also believing in and pursuing the future with hope.

To Change Your Day . . .

Remember:

- Hope triggers motivation and resilience. Do you see yourself as being hopeful? Do you have hope that you can grow your ability to thrive?

- Nobody can turn you into a Thriver but you.

- Thrivers see the six people out of seven, but focus on the one out of seven.

- Identify at least three people whom you consider to be your "heroes" when it comes to pursuing and sustaining change. What about their life inspires you? Do you truly believe that you can become like that person?

CHAPTER 4

Stay in the Day

"Andy, I have no balance in my life."

I was in Las Vegas and had just finished presenting a program on stress and work/life balance when Janet came to me with this statement. She had stayed after the presentation, and had stood near the auditorium exit while five or six other people had lined up to ask me questions. As I gathered my presentation notes and prepared to leave the auditorium, she came to stand directly in front of me. I looked up from gathering my things and said with surprise, "Oh, hi. Can I help you?" She responded, "Andy, I have no balance in my life. I've got to do something."

She then described the situation that had brought her to this realization.

Janet had been walking around a beautiful Cancun resort, scouting it out for her company's next executive retreat. She should have been enjoying her time there. Instead, she had sweated off all her makeup, was feeling embarrassed, and was silently praying that the site tour would end soon. She had stopped the group that was being escorted around the resort *five times* so that she might catch her breath.

It might have been the heat and humidity. It might have been the 47 pounds she had gained over the past four years. It might have been the stress she felt about her new responsibilities at work. Likely it was the "D" answer—all of the above.

Janet's increase in work responsibilities had resulted in her sleeping with her phone near her head so she could check for messages in the middle of the night. She barely recovered from one round of deadlines before the next project consumed her. She found that any mention of stress fell on deaf ears. Her friends, coworkers, and even her significant other thought of her job as being all first-class travel and champagne dreams.

It was true that Janet had wanted and had worked hard to attain her current position, but she had also come to realize that she had greatly underestimated how much the extra work and responsibilities would impact her. Her hair was thinning, she had been prescribed medication for high blood pressure, and her physician routinely told her that she needed to change her lifestyle.

Janet's family had initially been supportive of her longer hours at work and out-of-town business trips, but recently they had begun to complain about missing her, and also missing her formerly cheerful attitude. She rarely had the time to visit with friends, which is something she craved. Exercise? "Not a chance—no time." Date night? "That would be nice." Volunteer for good causes? "I'd like to."

As I took a breath to respond to her, she stopped me. "Andy, I will try whatever you suggest, *if* you can tell me when I will reach my goal of a more balanced life."

I am a researcher by background and educational training, so I responded in my research mode, "There are just too many variables to tell exactly *when*." In truth, this can be affected by variables in genetics, family history, personal life experiences. . . . She responded, "No, no, no, Andy. If I am going to try to change my life, I need to know *when* it will happen!"

I immediately recognized that Janet had fallen victim to a common mind-set. She was clearly thinking that she had to change her *life*. Her whole life. All simultaneously.

I tried to explain, as briefly as I could, that she needed to stop worrying about *when* she would see the big result she wanted. Rather, she needed to have faith that results *could* come and *would* come. But she wouldn't have any of that. "Andy, I want to know when, and I'm not going to do anything you tell me to do unless you can tell me how long it is going to take for my life to make some serious improvements."

I thought a moment, and then finally said, "Okay, Janet. If you do what I am going to suggest to you, you will achieve your goal of balance by June 31 of this year."

Her face brightened with excitement and then immediately darkened. "Andy, there are only 30 days in June," she said.

I wasn't trying to trick Janet or convey a message that I didn't think she would ever reach any of her goals in a timely manner. To the contrary, I was trying to get her to make a quick, abrupt, and vital change in her perspective.

I said, "Janet, you don't have to change your whole life. That is too big a goal. It's too hard to sustain multiple changes all at once. Trying that will suck the fun and motivation out of you. I want to help you *change your day*, not your whole life."

I readily admit that she stared at me blankly, but I could also tell that her mental wheels were turning. She agreed to meet with me to discuss the concept of changing her day.

Core Concept: Change Your Day

When I met next with Janet, I asked her to tell me about her typical workday.

Here is what she described:

Janet awoke to an alarm each morning, usually from a deep sleep. She instinctively hit the snooze button. Ring, snooze. Ring, snooze. Ring, groan, and finally she'd get up. Her first thought of the day was usually that she was running behind. She began rushing to get ready to leave her home, with no breakfast except perhaps something dispensed from a vending machine at her workplace on her way upstairs to her office.

She usually careened into her office with caffeine in hand, and she became a productivity machine as the caffeine kicked in. About an hour later, she usually had a sinking feeling of exhaustion, so she'd get up and set out for what she called a little "cubicle trick-or-treating," and if

(continued)

(continued)

that failed, she ended up in the break room to see if anyone had brought in doughnuts.

On the way back to her desk, she grabbed more java, which pushed the needle a little past "reasonable" caffeine intake. Her coffee, of course, was heavily laced with sugar and cream.

Shortly after she got back into full-productivity mode, it was time for lunch. For her, the choice between the "guiltless chicken breast" and the "loaded cheeseburger" was . . . well, it was no choice at all.

After lunch, although she tried to be highly productive, she often felt overdrawn in the energy department and with a correspondingly high level of stress. By mid-afternoon, she usually felt little desire to work even though she felt anxious about how much work she had. Rather than make an important phone call, for example, she would open up a web browser to do a little "Internet research," which was often not related to a work project.

Janet felt the added pressure that this deferral of key work meant that she was going to have to take more work home. That pattern had come to feel like the norm.

On the way home, she usually had moments of reflecting about how grateful she was to have her family. Even so, she admitted that she often began barking at them the minute she opened the door, and then almost immediately regretted her behavior.

By the time she sat down to dinner, the stress of the day fueled her into eating just about everything in sight, as if it was her last supper, which also created more internal struggles later—both physically and emotionally!

Finally, exhausted after knocking out most of the work she had brought home, she would collapse on her bed. As soon as her eyes were closed, however, her mind would wind up and begin to worry about the next day's to-do list. She often felt that she had just settled into deep, deep sleep when the alarm sounded and the routine began all over again.

A CONTINUAL CYCLE OF SABOTAGE

Before we go further, let me assure you that Janet's story is not a made-up story. She is a real person to whom I gave practical ideas. I worked with her for several months as she began to reengineer her day, a little bit at a time, so that she consistently built herself up to a routine that energized her, and that helped her achieve and sustain greater productivity, creativity, and good relationships with her coworkers and loved ones. We worked from a very basic premise: Don't try to change your whole life. Short-term goals and simple daily habits build upon one another. Remember, motivation is momentum in disguise.

Core Concept: Don't try to change your whole life. Short-term goals and simple daily habits build upon one another.

Initially, I felt that my major goal with Janet was to help her see that her daily patterns were consistently sabotaging her motivation and best-laid plans and goals. She had become stuck in a vicious cycle that de-energized her and made everything seem more difficult, both to achieve and to sustain.

It wasn't a matter of willpower, or a lack of willpower. She needed a better game plan—a better standard operating procedure. She needed to adopt a new pattern of simple daily behaviors that could help her build momentum. It was going to be these habitual daily behaviors that would be the key to taking her from where she was to where she wanted to be.

Most of all, I encouraged her, "You must stay in the day."

The choices need to be made daily. The behaviors need to be practiced daily. The rewards need to be felt in a day. And, if her day imploded, she could get back on track in a day.

(continued)

(continued)

That's the fastest way to build the momentum and to move a person consistently forward and upward to their highest aspirations.

Let me fast-forward.

Two years after my first encounter with Janet, I returned to Las Vegas to give a presentation to her corporation. After the presentation, four people lined up to talk with me. After I had spoken to the first two people, I turned to the third person and said, "May I answer a question for you?" There was a rather uncomfortable pause and then the woman before me asked, "What is today's date?"

I thought that question was a bit odd, but I replied, "March 22." She replied, "No, Andy, it is June 31."

I hadn't recognized Janet! During the two years since I had met with her, she had implemented the game plan I outlined for her and had lost nearly 75 pounds, putting her back into clothes she had not worn since college. She laughed because, to her amazement, those clothes at the back of her closet were back in style.

Her coworkers were amazed at the change in her life—not only her physical appearance, but the changes in her attitude, demeanor, and management skills.

Janet no longer gave people an "all access pass" to her time. Her new day had set work-life boundaries, time for uninterrupted work and time for herself, and these changes not only stuck but were met with far less resistance than she had initially anticipated. Her productivity, health, and optimism had never been at higher levels. Others around her also seemed to be on a path toward greater productivity, better health, and higher morale. Her team, in a down economy, had become the number one division when it came to reaching business goals. Janet was no longer striving for a better life. She was thriving on a day-by-day basis.

Janet finished our conversation that evening by telling me about another moment of truth. Again, she had been in Cancun.

This time, however, she had not struggled physically—she had actually climbed Chichen Itza to see the Mayan temple there. She said, "I didn't need to stop once on that steep hike." She went on, "Andy, I live each day now with more hope, more energy, more motivation, and greater confidence that I'm doing what I want to do. I'm reaching my daily personal goals. I cannot tell you how much of a difference it made when you switched my focus from feeling a need to change my life to changing my day. I stay in the day now. And staying in the day, and changing my day, has changed my life."

The change may be almost imperceptible. But the truth is, the change is occurring in the person who seeks to change daily patterns of behavior. The changes in physical behavior, attitude, thinking, motivational level, feelings, and relationships build upon one another. They produce subtle benefits and tiny bits of growth, which begin to accumulate in truly amazing ways.

Perhaps most important of all, a decision to stay in the day takes pressure off most people when it comes to the massive amount of changes they think they need to make in order to be more of whatever they desire to be more of! More successful. More healthy. More personable. More loving. More educated. More accomplished. More fit. Whatever it is that becomes the desired "more" goal, that goal begins to be achieved—but without pressure and without undue striving—if a person scales the goal back to the day.

Janet made herself one of the one in seven who is conscientious, works hard, and truly brings about change in her life. She gives me hope! She is a Thriver! She is a hard-working, responsible adult with a strong desire to succeed and accepts responsibility for her own life. She is willing to sacrifice some things for the success she desires, but she is not sacrificing what is truly valuable to her. As a Thriver, she has found a "way of life" that enfolds both her time at work and her time away from work.

THE PARADOX OF GAINING MORE WITH LESS EFFORT

When I meet people like Janet—and when I see the tremendous results in their lives that are the product of shifting their focus to daily behaviors and habits, I have a much brighter view of the world. I gain hope. I see thriving played out fully, and have a renewed sense that far more people are capable of thriving than are presently doing so.

An older, wiser friend once said to me, "Life doesn't need to be as hard as many people make it."

I believe that is true on a number of levels.

Problems abound. I'm not in denial about that.

Challenges in our world are big.

But nearly all problems, challenges, and needs are best faced if they are brought down the scale of "what can be done right now" by taking on "one small piece" of a difficult situation.

Doing everything all at once simply isn't possible. And it isn't healthful.

Doing something positive in a daily context is possible. And it is not only healthful, but highly beneficial over time.

Bit by bit.

Step by step.

Day by day.

And then one piece at a time fits together into your day so you can tap into the vast amounts of energy and ability inside you.

Who, me? you may be thinking.

Yes! Almost every psychological theory about human nature says in one form or another that you DO have a vast amount of energy and ability, and you are capable of doing far more than you presently are doing while, at the same time, absorbing less stress. Read on!

To Change Your Day . . .

Remember:

- Thrivers don't try to change their whole life. They know the value of determining and defining what is DOable in a day. They put a lot of value on "generational growth." Discrete, small, doable behaviors add up to make a day satisfying or unsatisfying. The defining of those behaviors is up to you. And so are definitions for "satisfying" and "unsatisfying." Remember to Stay in the Day!

What are you capable of adjusting in your daily habits? What might you change in the first hour of your day? What might you change in the first half hour after you get home? What might you change in the last 15 minutes before you fall asleep?

CHAPTER 5

The Big Picture of Balance

"Balance" is not a goal only for Janet. It is a word heard often in today's workplace, especially in motivational circles. Some people call it work/life balance or work/life integration. Scott Heiferman, CEO at MeetUp, said, "I'm not into the phrase work/life balance, exactly. But, however you want to phrase it, it is a really important thing." I couldn't say it better myself.

Work/life balance is usually expressed as an example of synergy, a key factor in effectiveness, with an end goal of happiness and fulfillment.

At a recent conference at which I was scheduled to speak, the event organizer removed the word "balance" from my biography as she prepared the brochure. She told me that her people "react negatively" to the word. When I probed as to why the word "balance"—which I see as a big positive—could be regarded as a negative, she replied, "Many people feel guilty for not already having balance in their lives, and the rest don't think it is possible. A few don't think the concept even exists."

I'm often challenged on Twitter with comments on how balance is impossible. For example, one tweet I received read, "@andycore @Forbes—don't see the reason: weight of silver and lead have different weight—therefore you need different amounts to balance."

Like Scott Heiferman's quote, I too believe that balance is a really important thing, but the problem is in how people define it. My response to the challenging tweet was: "50/50 #balance, if possible, would underdeliver. I love your silver/lead metaphor. #balance is ~ synergy, 1+1=3."

I suggest that those people start seeing the one in seven, because in my experience, most people DO believe balance, in one definition or another, exists, even though they admit they don't have it, and they're not at all sure how to achieve it or if it possible to achieve it and be "successful" in today's working world.

I get it. From a purely objective perspective, a state of balance implies equilibrium, and in most areas of life, equilibrium sucks the passion out of life and creates a status quo that is less energetic, less dynamic, and more likely to produce resistance than motivation.

Even so, I often hear:

- My work is consuming me, and my family is suffering.
- I'm succeeding at my job and failing in my health and non-work relationships.
- I'm not sure all the time and energy that I'm pouring into my career is going to be worth it in 40 years.

But, what should you do if you are passionate about becoming more successful and/or often challenged to accomplish more, faster, better and in less time than before? How do you "balance" a high-demand job with the needs for fulfilling personal relationships, maintaining your health, and having a high quality of life?

First, let me suggest a change in terms. Let's take the approach of Tony Hsieh, CEO of Zappos and author of *Delivering Happiness*, who has written, "Rather than focus on work/life separation or work/life balance, I think it's more important to focus on work/life integration. People should be doing what they're passionate about doing, and having fun doing it. At the end of the day, it shouldn't be about work vs. life—it should just be about life."

I agree fully. Integration means that work and life are complementary—they work together in concert to fuel who you are and who you want to become.

Second, let me state that I believe that when work is integrated fully into a high-quality LIFE, a 1 + 1 = 3 formula kicks in. The key is to seek an enhancement of *all* of life that moves a person's existence into a stratum of excellence. In this stratum, mind, emotions, and body are energized so that whatever is *done*—whether a task, a conversation, a performance, a practice session, the reading of a bedtime story, a one-on-one pickup game of basketball, a time of learning or prayer—the *doing* is a high-quality performance. Segments of doing that are high quality tend to build on one another. All of life takes on an atmosphere of excellence.

THE STRATUM OF EXCELLENCE

One of my favorite quotes is a statement made by former U.S. President John F. Kennedy. When he was asked to define "happiness," he said, "The full use of your powers along lines of excellence."

Excellence is doing what you are gifted to do—what you have talents to do, innate propensities to do, and skills to do. Using your gifts to the best of your ability—and ultimately at a high level of ability—is a mark of excellence. And in that there is tremendous joy, fulfillment, and a deep sense of satisfaction. If you want to be "happy," do your best at all times. You may not be the best in the world at what you are doing, but you are in the process of becoming the best you can be, and increasingly better at what you do.

The key to developing a total life of excellence is rooted in the pervasive nature of one's values, goals, dreams, and beliefs. Work/life integration is not primarily about achieving a ratio of work to personal time, as it is a composite expression of a purposeful, fulfilling life that exhibits the finest character qualities.

We are back to DO-KNOW-BE. When a person is doing his or her best at all hours of a day, expressing fully his or her values and beliefs in a consistent manner, a habit is forged that produces character. Life becomes integrated. What is held to be true, good, and virtuous in one setting . . . is true, good, and virtuous in all settings. There is no switching from "work mode" or "work values" to "home mode" and "home values."

What does it take to live an integrated life?

- A well-defined and focused set of values and beliefs.
- A desire for excellence.
- An ability to choose tasks, responsibilities, memberships, and associations that are complementary.
- An ability to delegate and manage life as a whole.

The first two factors above require a person to do some internal work. You must decide what it is that you truly believe and value. You must choose excellence.

The last two factors are part of a personal Strategic Operating Procedure. A fully integrated person makes choices about tasks, associations, responsibilities, and memberships on the basis of how well these obligations of time and energy fit together easily and productively. A fully integrated person becomes the CEO of his or her life. Many of the same skills required to be a successful executive or manager on the job from nine to five are put into play to take on the management of life 24/7.

YOU ARE THE CEO OF YOU

Most people seem to relegate the concept of *management* to a work environment, or to work relationships. Management, however, by definition, is the process of organizing and controlling all available resources—time, materials, money, and personnel—to successfully reach a goal or maintain a desired level of quality. Management includes plenty of communication and rewards. It includes such things as goal statements and vision statements.

And in the realm of all of life, each of these aspects of management ultimately happens consciously or subconsciously.

Think about a family. Think about a marriage. Think about a life devoted to service. Think about the way you integrate with your community.

Every aspect of your life is ultimately subjected to a "budget"—the use of your resources. Every aspect of life includes other people, since no person truly can gain significance as a lone ranger. Every aspect of life includes allocations of time, energy, talents, and nonfinancial tangible resources. If this is true, and I believe it to be, then with work-life integration each of your successes fully fuels the other areas of your life.

Keith Ferrazi, author of *Who's Got Your Back* and *Never Eat Alone*, said, "Everything you have achieved in life has been achieved by the help of others. Every dream you will achieve will happen with other people." I have this quote on my office wall. I look at it and try to live by it daily. But even so, you are the CEO of your life. You get to make the decisions.

One of my friends is a professional therapist, and when I feel like giving him a hard time, I'll say, "And how do you feel about that?" to many of his comments. Kidding aside, he is a great therapist and a master of questions. He skillfully asks questions in a specific sequence. As you think about and answer them, you—often abruptly—come to the realization that where you are in life right now is a result of your decisions. That you are more in control of your decisions, thoughts, and future than you might believe. After this thought settles into your mind, it becomes an empowering and wonderfully motivating ideal.

When you begin to think strategically about the whole of your life, and take on the role of CEO of your life, you likely will find that some things don't fully fuel the other areas of life. If something does not, it is extraneous and should be phased out or jettisoned immediately in order to streamline your overall "life operation." Other things may need to be folded into your schedule, your budget, and your set of responsibilities in order for you truly to max out what you perceive to be your purpose in life. The end goals are subject to your design, but I suspect you likely will place high value on quality health (emotional, physical, and spiritual), a sense of fulfillment, and deep happiness or joy. In that framework, money becomes a tool to reach goals, not the end game.

The CEO of a total life is going to be a person who knows that play and rest are vital to performance—both personal relaxation and recreation, as well as team-related retreats and experiences with others. I like what George Santayana once said: "To the art of working well a civilized race would add the art of playing well."

In this scenario of total life management, balance is a byproduct. It is essential, but it is not the first consideration. The first considerations are always values and beliefs, an integration of character across all tasks, and a goal of excellence in all performances.

Doing less, and doing it well, can elevate excellence.

Doing less and involving others can elevate morale and reduce stress.

Doing all things with a sense of "get to" instead of "have to" can produce greater motivation.

As the CEO of your life, you get to define what works for you, and what doesn't. And with that perspective, your hours at a job or in a workplace become aspects of a *whole life* subject to your control.

In no way do I downplay the need to work hard to become successful. Neither do I dismiss the need to "put in the hours" that success demands. Hard work is a must in every area of life . . . but let's define "hard." Hard work is consistent effort marked by creativity, wise choices and decisions, and focused energy. All of these—creative output, decision-making, and the allocation of energy—are management decisions. They are also aspects of a successful marriage, family life, and enriching friendships. Marriage, parenting, and friendships also require creativity, wise choices and decisions, and focused energy. The good CEO of his or her life considers all factors, and allocates accordingly across all dimensions of life.

A strategic operating plan is the *vehicle* for engineering success, and along the way, integrating all factors of life.

WHAT WON'T YOU SACRIFICE?

A major factor to consider in work/life integration is found in the answer you give to this question: "What are you *unwilling* to sacrifice?"

We all know the stories of those who worked hard and achieved the top rung of their respective ladder only to find that they had a trail of personal debris in their wake— damaged relationships, poor health, and a void deep inside that begged to know "Is this all there is?"

The pursuit of goals may require sacrifice of bits and pieces from time to time. There may be less time for the pursuit of hobbies, less "alone" time, less time for shopping for the latest gadget, and so forth. But no goal is worth the sacrifice of any- thing that a person deems to be *eternally* important or part of what makes life meaningful and fulfilling. Perhaps it might be worth the sacrifice for a week or two, but be careful to not let this sacrifice become your standard operating procedure (SOP)!

Core Concept: Pick Three

Amy Jo Martin, author of *Renegades Write the Rules*, once found her- self sitting in a meeting that did not directly involve her areas of responsibility. She became a bit bored and mentally began running through her mental to-do list. She tried to look interested, but realized that she hadn't succeeded when her boss, who was seated next to her, handed her a note. On it were three words: Work. Family. Self.

After she read the note, her boss leaned over and whispered, "Pick two."

She could tell that Amy Jo didn't fully understand what she was saying, so she added, "To really be successful here, you have to pick two."

(continued)

(*continued*)

At that very moment, although she knew she was considered one of the company's most talented "up and comers," Amy Jo mentally quit her job. Two months later, she made it an official resignation. Soon after, she began her own company, which soon became one of the most successful in her industry. She said, "I picked three. I was not only more successful, but happier. I had more energy, more patience, and was more motivated than I had been in years."

Can a person truly pick all three?

Yes.

And please note that even if you do not have a family—perhaps you are not married, or are married and have no children—you still have a family. You likely have parents, siblings, or close relations. You may be invested emotionally in godchildren or nieces and nephews. And for many people, friends are definitely members of the family.

"Pick three" applies to all people.

To Change Your Day . . .

Remember:

- Thrivers see balance, however they define it, less as the reward of a successful life and more as the vehicle that makes lasting success possible. They believe that work + life is $1 + 1 = 3$.

- Thrivers are the CEO of their life. They are in control of how they manage their life, and do so based on their values, character, and a goal of excellence in all performances.

- Thrivers know what they are not willing to sacrifice. What is sacred to you?

CHAPTER 6

Jettison the Junk Hours

The chairman of the board of one of the top trucking companies in the United States has one of the sharpest minds and the most business experience I have encountered. He hired me to help one of his leaders. He described him as "a super-hard worker, dedicated, with great potential." The CEO was worried about him, however, because he was showing signs of burnout, and was not taking care of himself physically. He had recently let his weight get above the 280-pound mark. The CEO said, "I'm worried he will burn himself out before he reaches his potential."

After we finished discussing how to help this employee, I said, "I know that you have an army of young, smart, and dedicated workers under you—all of whom are aiming to climb the success ladder at your company. They each want to be on the top team. What do you think is the main difference between the ones who are going to make it, and the ones who won't?" I had expected him to respond with the answers I have heard often: hard work, dedication, passion, innovation.

Instead, he said, "I have met very few truly successful people in my career. They all seem to be clearly focused and adamant about having some form of balance in their life."

I asked him to give me a description of a "balanced" career person. He replied, "These are people who work exceptionally hard, and often exceptionally long hours, but no matter how long or hard they work, they remain sharp, focused, and eager to face a new challenge or capture a new opportunity. I've decided that the difference between these employees and most of the others is that they have learned to work fewer 'junk' hours."

IDENTIFY AND ELIMINATE THE JUNK

What is a "junk hour"?

Well, it's a little like junk food. Junk food may taste good, but it provides no real nutrition to the body, and actually can deplete energy rather than provide or sustain energy. Junk food often offers short-term pleasure and long-term exhaustion.

Junk hours may or may not seem to be "fun" in the moment, but they produce no significant productivity, and often push real work beyond the workday and into the night. Junk hours can be spent chasing rabbit trails on the Internet, with colleagues at the water cooler, with a few jokes and laughs, but they do not genuinely build friendships or enhance work skills. Junk hours can sometimes be spent in meetings that are not necessary, acquiring information that is not essential to doing high-quality work.

Junk hours are going through the motions of work, but no real *work* is being done—and in nearly all cases, the person knows it even if his or her boss doesn't. The person is putting in the time, but not gaining a real sense of satisfaction or fulfillment from what is being done.

In health and productivity research this is called presenteeism. Basically, you are physically at work, but your mind is absent.

For a person to truly sustain motivation and build maximum success, the junk hours need to be eliminated.

But what goes into their "time slot"?

The answer lies in the very reason that many people seek out junk activities at work. In Janet's case, she was bored and likely was experiencing an energy low from too much sugar earlier in the day. For others, a little play on the Internet helps lower the immediate stress related to a deadline. If a person can isolate WHY they are engaging in junk hours, they nearly always can look a little deeper to discover what WILL give them the break from routine that they desire, but in a way that BUILDS work productivity and satisfaction rather than depletes it.

TIME EXCHANGES

Ben was greatly admired in his company. In fact, his company's training department was using him as an example to teach others and to initiate new hires. Ben had an amazing work ethic: He was focused, a smart risk taker, and a bold thinker.

Ben, unfortunately, experienced a real health scare. He said, "There's nothing quite like feeling that a vise grip has clamped down on your heart, and thinking that you are going to die, to get you to do a little reflective thinking."

Ben was highly competitive and he knew, as he reflected on his life and goals, that he *liked* being competitive. He enjoyed his work. He liked playing—and winning—the "business game." At the same time, he loved his family and wanted to be alive to see his children finish college, marry, and give him grandkids to love.

Ben was smart enough to know that he *didn't* know how to restructure his life. He went to his company's practice-management expert, and he was fortunate that the practice-management person in his corporation had also experienced a health scare and was focused on improving business strategies that *also* helped people improve their overall life strategies.

He and Ben worked together to streamline some of Ben's work tasks and develop a daily strategy so that he had built-in time for recharging himself physically. In other words, Ben was shown ways he could carve out time to exercise . . . and to continue to get all his work goals met in the process.

Ben adopted a new routine.

He got up each morning and spent some time journaling while he ate a healthy breakfast. Twice a week he arranged to meet with friends—on Tuesdays he spent his lunch hour play-ing racquetball with an old friend, rather than squeezing in more work between bites of a burger. Most Thursday nights he and his wife spent time socializing with a small group of friends.

Since Ben was able to structure his own work schedule, including time in the office and out of the office, he was able to set aside one hour on Mondays, Wednesdays, and Fridays to go to a gym about two blocks from his office. He walked there, changed into workout clothes, spent a full 30 minutes on a treadmill or in the swimming pool, showered, dressed, and walked back to his office—60 minutes total. After writ-ing appointments and meetings on his calendar, he added his "appointments with Jim" (Jim and "gym" were one and the same).

Ben found that the exercise hours actually increased both his energy levels and sense of well-being to the point that he was able to work faster and smarter the rest of each work-day. His overall average workweeks went from 65–70 hours to 40–45 hours, depending on the week.

Did this adjustment in Ben's schedule impact his income?

Only in a positive way! He actually began to post higher sales figures.

MORE PRODUCTIVITY PER HOUR

In most cases, the elimination of junk hours causes an almost automatic increase in work productivity. In Ben's case, exer-cise hours gave him time to "clear his mind" and he often found that on his walk back to his office, new ideas filled his mind and he had something of a second wind for turning those ideas into workable goals and plans.

Junk hours don't simply waste time. They tend to DISTRACT a person—or perhaps DETOUR a person or

DISSIPATE his or her energy and focus. What is done in junk hours squanders innovation and creativity. A person may think he or she is "just taking a break," but in truth, that break is truly a *break in momentum*!

When a person chooses to "take a break," he or she must make a key decision: What can I do that will produce something positive—something beneficial, something rewarding, something energizing? The replacement for a junk hour must be an hour that continues to build motivation and momentum. There must be a sense of accomplishment for something related to the person's overall life goals and values.

IT ISN'T ALL ABOUT MONEY

Jim Komoszewski was the first vice president and director of a strategic business unit at National Planning Corporation (NPC). He told me: "In our business, it is easy to become a workaholic. Our people start their careers gung ho. They have an entrepreneurial spirit. They like helping others build a financially secure life and, in the process, obtaining success for themselves. Some of them have significant egos. And a high percentage seem to think, 'I can put the rest of my life on hold, and then after I make a ton of money I can use it to fix any aspects of my life that need fixing.'

"But," Jim continued, "in our coaching program, I have found that not one of my top producers asks me how to make more money. Rather, what they really want to talk with me about is how they can get more of their life back. How they can work fewer hours so they might have more time for nonwork activities, and yet still make the same income. We have lots of strategies for helping people work smarter. Some have been able to reduce their work hours by as much as 30 percent and, at the same time, *increase* their income."

I recently heard about a man who had become a widower and had attempted to sustain the double-entry ledger system of his wife in keeping the books for his own finances, which were far less complicated than the finances his wife had managed when their business was at its peak. He went to an accountant and said, "How do I do this? How do I keep track of the information *you* need in order to prepare my taxes?" He came away from a two-hour meeting greatly relieved. The task of bookkeeping was manageable and understandable. It was only going to take three hours a month. He could simplify the system and lose nothing important!

That should be the goal for every person. The way you learned "at the beginning"—of either of a particular job or the start of your career—may not be the best strategy for you NOW. Find out the optimum WAY of doing what you need to do.

Think about what you can do to become as:

- Efficient as you can be—taking as few steps as necessary.
- Fast and error-free as you can be—taking up as little time as necessary.
- Productive as you can be—juggling and completing as many tasks as you can in a particular day.
- Streamlined as you can be—eliminating all wasted motion.

Work with someone who knows the ropes of good time and task management.

The byproduct of a new and more efficient way of working is likely going to be less boredom and less need to seek out the "distractions" of junk hour activities.

Jim told me that those who build in "health" activities to replace junk hours often see as much as a 42 percent improvement in their business. The health activity might be anything from an exercise break in a formal gym to a walking meeting in place of a "sit-down" to a run around a park across the street. It might be a "mental health" break that still produces something that is valuable to the employee.

I recently met a woman who takes a 20-minute knitting break every day, usually at 2 o'clock. She said, "I drink a big jug of ice water and pull my knitting out of the file drawer and let the needles fly. I always have a project in process—usually a gift and sometimes a baby blanket for a homeless shelter around the corner. This is a total break in my work routine. I am focused on the hand-eye coordination project before me. I have a sense of accomplishment at the end of the 20 minutes that I am one step closer to the completion of something that has value and beauty, and is of benefit to others. Doing *handwork* gives me a genuine mental break, and it is actually rather amazing, Andy. On many days, I find that as my fingers are engaged in something practical and rhythmic, my mind actually shifts gears and I come away with a new idea, or a new insight into the work project I'm doing. I'm ready to get back to work, and with a sense of fulfillment. Over time, 20 minutes of knitting ends up being almost seven hours of knitting a month—and that very often is a completed item. Accomplishment!"

This woman is maintaining momentum in less time than most people take a coffee break, keeping her mind engaged, and producing something in line with what is important to the whole of her life. This is the exact opposite of a junk hour!

There are countless ways to exchange junk hours for hours that build greater health and value into a workday. Jim told me, "I've coached more than 120 advisors and discovered more than 120 ways to find a more productive balance between work and the whole of life. There are countless ways to work smarter, and to work smarter for the WHOLE of a person's life."

To Change Your Day . . .

Remember:

- Thrivers work fewer junk hours, which gives them time to maintain or improve their physical and emotional health, which in turn fuels greater work performance.
- Be honest with yourself and own up to your junk hours.

What might you replace them with?
What activities will give you a break from your work routine and at the same time

- Improve your physical health?
- Improve your emotional or mental health?
- Increase your creativity?
- Help you sustain momentum and motivation?

Seek to jettison the junk hours and at the same time add value and fun to your day!

CHAPTER 7

Greater Self-Awareness

Jeff is a local sports legend. He is the past captain of a university "dream team," the only one to win a national championship in the state's history for his sport. Even now, decades after he graduated, most local restaurants won't let him pay for a meal. They are proud he has chosen their place of business!

Jeff was drafted to the pros and had a successful career, and then he went to medical school and eventually became a well-known surgeon in his home community.

When Jeff approached me for personal coaching, I was not at all sure how, or if, I could help him. He seemed to have lived, and to be living, an exceptional life. Over coffee Jeff said, "Andy, I've reached a lot of goals, but there is so much more I want to do, and feel a need to do. My focus, energy, and motivation are often not what I want them to be."

Jeff was struggling a little with the answer to a longstanding question of many successful people: "Why don't I always do what I know I should do . . . and even *want* to do?"

The answer to that question, I believe, begins with an understanding of the basics of our collective lives.

AT OUR CORE

I hope you will find it encouraging to realize that we human beings are far more alike than we are different.

Nearly all of us want to help others, be connected to others, be active and healthy, and we all want to accomplish things in life and be valued for what we achieve.

We are all born with an extraordinary ability and innate motivation to learn, love, help, and live. Most of us want to improve ourselves—in various ways—for our entire life.

We have DNA that is 99 percent alike! We are far more alike as human beings than we are different, even if we are of different races and gender.

Just think about it . . . unless you have had an accident, surgery, or were born with a specific abnormality . . . You have a spleen. I have a spleen.

Our spleens are in the same place in our bodies and function in pretty much the same way.

You have fingernails. I have fingernails.

You have two ears, located on either side of your head. So do I.

Our similarities abound anatomically, physiologically, and in behavioral ways that are hard to define fully.

Perhaps our greatest similarity is that we are finite creatures living in a world of infinite possibilities and combinations, and all of that is spread against a backdrop of history, the current moment, and eternity.

Furthermore . . .

We all live in a world in which the sun rises and sets each day. We all have a basic routine that involves waking, eating, working, and sleeping.

And most people seem to have some difficulty—at least at some point in their lives—staying motivated, energized, and focused.

The question "Why don't I do what I *want* to do?" is a very common question asked by the vast majority of people! Thrivers and Strivers both suffer from it.

There are two answers that I encourage people to explore.

The first answer lies in a greater awareness of your uniqueness. Even though you are mostly like the rest of humanity, you are also one of a kind.

You are a composite of hundreds of factors that are aligned and proportionately unique. Explore your uniqueness. It holds many clues as to *why* you don't stay as focused and energized as you *want* to be.

KNOW YOUR RHYTHM AND CAPACITY

Are you aware that even one-cell organisms, such as bacteria, have a built-in 24-hour rhythm?

The flow of energy is universal, and while we are mostly alike, we each have a distinctive flow of energy, often called a biorhythm. Some people are night owls. Others are early birds.

Some people need nine hours of sleep a night to function at their best. Others do well with seven.

Some people process certain nutrients more efficiently and quickly than others—they have a higher metabolism, or lower metabolism, than the "norm."

Every person faces the challenge in a day of discovering their optimal biological rhythm, and then living within that rhythm for maximum productivity, energy, and effectiveness.

In addition to the rhythms of a day, we have a built-in human rhythm when it comes to a week. We are creatures who *need* times of relaxation every week in order to stay at our best.

Think moon cycles and the rising and falling of tides according to the fullness of the moon! Our bodies are mostly water, subject to the pull of gravity, and it only makes sense that certain biorhythms are impacted by gravitational forces that we rarely give pause to consider.

And frankly, most of us are not in touch with our bodies to the point that we fully recognize all that influences us. There is very often a physical reason for our lack of energy—and that can be a direct cause for our lack of ability to remain focused and motivated. We are wise to get in touch with ourselves, not in order to blame our choices and behavior on physical or natural causes, but to be aware of these influences so that we can take evasive or compensatory steps!

In addition to the general way in which each of us is a unique one-of-a-kind entity, we also face unique circumstances and situations. We have a one-of-a-kind litany of events and encounters, and each event or encounter has a physical and emotional impact on our energy and motivation.

People recovering from a major accident or illness . . .
People reeling from an unexpected or unwanted divorce . . .
People grieving the loss of a loved one . . .

. . . Are all people who are likely *not* going to be able to do all they want to do or believe they should do. They need to cut themselves some temporary slack, and take concerted measures to rebuild their physical and emotional reserves so they can restore, renew, and rehabilitate their own reserves of energy and strength. They need to seek out extra measures of restoring their spiritual and emotional health. They need to pay special attention to the root causes for their lack of motivation.

Back to Jeff. As a surgeon, he sometimes found himself at a hospital for as long as 40 hours at a stretch without sleep. He did his best to control his schedule, and to eat and sleep with as much regularity as possible, but his schedule did not always seem to be his "own" to manage.

Core Concept: Manage what you can manage.

The challenge is to manage what you *can* manage. Start there. Managing what you can manage is often enough to compensate for what you cannot manage.

In seeking to manage your day, and to make changes that will occur daily, you need to address how your particular body is wired. Know your rhythms and know your capacities.

How much food do you actually need in a day?
How much water?
How much sleep?

How much of which nutrients do you need—and if you are lacking in some vital nutrients, do you know which ones and how to get them?

Are you exercising daily, and sufficiently, to release stress and gain strength?

Are you taking medications in the right dosages?

Most charts related to height, weight, and physical capacity are based upon averages.

A five-foot three-inch woman and a six-foot seven-inch man should *not* be consuming the same calories, or taking medications at identical dosages!

Are you in sync with what you need to *sustain* a positive, upbeat outlook on life?

These are questions only you can answer, but they are questions worthy of answering! Part of the reason you don't do what you *want* to do may have to do with very practical physiological functions in your body.

The above factors related to food, sleep, exercise, and medications are things you *can* manage. Start there.

The facts associated with your unique physical and emotional make-up should always be taken into consideration as you move to part two of the "answer" related to focus and motivation: your decision-making skills.

DECISIONS AND CHOICES

I recently heard about a man who said, "Life is a series of decisions and their consequences."

While I don't know anyone who would disagree with that statement, few people seem to see that their personal life, in any given day, often boils down to a series of sequential choices and decisions . . . and their consequences.

In many cases, the choices and decisions not only produce immediate consequences, but one of the foremost consequences is that choices and decisions build upon one another and, in many ways, "prescribe" future choices and decisions.

A choice is a decision, and all decisions involve choices. In a broad sense, choices and decisions are good or bad because of the outcomes they produce.

Stop to consider . . .

When you go to bed at night, do you choose to watch late-night television, or do you turn off the light and go to sleep?

When you wake in the morning, what are your first thoughts? How are you choosing to think?

When you arrive at work, what is the first action you take? Are you prepared to launch into high-value work or do you allow a slow start?

In the break room at work, do you grab a doughnut or a Greek yogurt?

At the department store, do you buy a new gadget "on a whim" or keep your money in your pocket in anticipation of something you have been saving for?

Do you leave work with thoughts of what you've accomplished or what remains undone?

Upon arriving home from work, do you launch into dinner, eating like it's the end of the world, or do you lace on your walking shoes and go for a walk?

Do you respond to your significant other, pet, or child with patience . . . or impatience?

All of these questions point to very simple routine choices and decisions that people make every day, often without genuine intention or forethought.

A high percentage of people react to life. They go with the flow around them and make instant choices without pausing to consider consequences or long-term impacts.

The key bit of awareness required of you is recognizing your own decision-making style the unique factors that surround your choices.

Are your choices made on a foundation of solid values and beliefs?

Is your decision-making reactionary or intentional and thoughtful as you make choices?

Have you developed an attitude of "what will be, will be," or do you firmly believe that "what will be is related to who I am and what I decide"?

YOU DO KNOW THE RIGHT CHOICES TO MAKE

Let me give you a ray of encouragement. People who ask, "Why don't I do what I want to do, or what I know I should do?" are admitting at one level that they DO know the right things to do. That's a big plus! A truly clueless person doesn't ask, "Why don't I do what I desire to do?" A truly thoughtless person doesn't question his or her lack of focus or motivation.

So give yourself some solid points on this account.

Through my years of coaching and researching working adults in a variety of disciplines, I have often asked clients these three questions:

1. To be better at work and in your personal life, do you know what you might do or should do?

   Every person has said "yes."

2. Do you know why you aren't doing the activities you should do at a level you could do them?

   Again, *every* person has said "yes." They gave different answers, but each person identified at least one reason why they weren't doing what they knew they could do or should do. Some said lack of time, some cited lack of money, some saw themselves as too tired or physically sick, and a few blamed another person for standing in their way.

3. Do you know someone who has less time and faces greater challenges, and yet still does what you could or should do to a greater degree of regularity than you?

Again, *every* person has said "yes!"

Including Jeff. I'm not going to tell you what Jeff's answers were, but let me assure you that once we got down to this level of analysis, Jeff clearly already knew what he needed to do in order to live the life he was pursuing.

Socrates once said, "My way toward the truth is to ask the right questions." I'm with Socrates. So the question I now ask as "question number four" is this: "To what degree do you want to be focused, motivated, healthy, and successful?" And question number five is a quick follow-up: "To what degree do you think you deserve to be or can be more focused, motivated, healthy, or successful?"

You can add any other objective of your choice to that list. You might add wealthy, educated, in a loving relationship, spiritually strong, influential, or any number of other traits or goals.

Do you think you are capable of having that, doing that, or becoming that? Do you think you are worthy of something greater, finer, more beneficial?

From my years of personal coaching, I have concluded that a primary reason many people have trouble staying focused and motivated tends to be because they don't believe they *can* do something, receive something, or earn something they think they need. And in other cases, they don't believe they *deserve* a brighter tomorrow.

The net result of thinking that you can't change or that you shouldn't receive greater rewards is the same: people give up before they reach their goals.

THE SELF-DETERMINATION THEORY

One of my favorite theories related to self-motivation, will-power, and "overcoming procrastination" is called the Self-Determination Theory. This theory contends that a person's innate nature is to be motivated, optimistic, and productive. If a person doesn't feel that way, then the person is simply not getting what he or she needs.

Unsatisfied needs create powerful and invisible barriers that stand between what a person wants to be and what he perceives that he is, or is capable of being. The greater the need, and the longer it goes unmet, the greater the force against the person—pushing him back, holding him down, or keeping him from making what seems to be an increasingly difficult effort.

Unmet needs hammer at our basic sense of self-worth and value. For a person to attempt to meet a need, that person must first believe that he is worthy of having the need met, and that the need *can* be met.

Without those basic beliefs, the person will not *try, at least not fully*. In not trying, he negates any hope of having the need met.

The good news is that when a person starts to satisfy more of the basic needs he feels, the more these barriers turn into stepping stones! The meeting of needs compels a person to seek to address and conquer more needs. A positive force is put into motion.

> **Core Concept: Positive motion creates positive emotion.**

To Change Your Day . . .

Remember:

- Before you will take steps to change your day, you must believe that you can change your day, and believe that when you do you will deserve to have a better day.

- What you decide will set you up to make choices and decisions that you *can* make, and that only you can make.

- Thrivers and Strivers alike suffer the question, "Why don't I do what I know I should and want to do?" Thrivers just have a better mental approach and daily system that fuels their motivational needs.

If you are willing to try, then you need to take these three steps:

1. Reflect on your own make-up and the rhythms of life that impact you. Do a little self-analysis that includes:

   - Identifying the "best" times of day for your most productive and creative work

   - Identifying your own flow of physical energy during a day

   - Identifying any prevailing external factors that may be sapping your energy or preoccupying your mind and emotions—either temporary or semipermanent factors

2. Make a list of three things you know you should do *every day*.

3. Make a list of changes you think might be made to ensure that you get those changes accomplished daily.

Nobody knows you as well as *you*.

CHAPTER **8**

The Pursuit of Patterns

All options that appear on our path in life eventually compel us to make a decision. Failing to make a decision *is* a decision . . . to not choose.

When it comes to changes we want to make—whether at work, in the status of our physical or emotional health, in our finances, in our relationships, or in any other area of life—we each inevitably reach a point where we must decide to try, and then specifically decide what we will DO.

I call these decision points mini moments of truth. These are like little personal flash points that reveal to us what we must do if we want to move forward in life.

The overarching truth is that we do not make choices in a vacuum. Various forces come into play that lead us to favor one choice over another, and to transform the choices we make into real-life behaviors.

The fork in the road is rarely like Robert Frost's two roads diverging in a yellow wood. Rather, we nearly always face a three-pronged decision-making fork:

1. Yes, proceed, make the change.
2. No, ignore the opportunity to change, maintain the status quo.
3. Wait and check again later.

In other terms, we face a moment when we take action, stay put, or procrastinate (putting off a decision or the taking of action).

Let me insert a word about procrastination.

There are times when it is wise to wait in making a decision or choice that involves others, or that is related to a work task. It may not be the right time to set a goal, sell a stock, buy a company, or launch a particular campaign in the work arena or in any other community venture or organization. However, when it comes to the setting of one's personal agenda and charting one's daily patterns, there is rarely a legitimate reason *not* to begin.

But, you may say, I can't exercise right now because I have a torn muscle. In truth, you can exercise in ways that don't require that muscle to be at full strength.

But, you may say, I can't get up an hour earlier to get a jump start on my day. In truth, you can set the alarm for an hour earlier and make a corresponding decision to go to bed an hour earlier at night.

I could give numerous examples, but you get the point. There is always something you can do today to start making progress, to start building momentum.

Therefore, in the realm of making personal choices to improve and decisions related to changing your day, procrastination is essentially a "no" decision. The fork in the road at the personal decision-making level regarding personal change is nearly always a clear-cut yes or no choice. You will choose to make a change, or you won't.

There is, however, a three-pronged model that is appropriate for personal change and it applies to virtually everybody. It is rooted in the research of B. J. Fogg, a noted behavior-change researcher and professor at Stanford University. He believes that there are three things necessary for a person to take action:

- Motivation
- Ability
- Trigger
- M + A + T = ACTION

All three must be present simultaneously.

For example, if you are tired of being stressed and rushed in the mornings and you desire a calmer and more positive morning routine, you are wise to consider waking up 30 minutes earlier. For this to happen:

- You must have a motivating reason to do something. (It may be that you've missed one too many commuter trains or that you have left behind something important on too many mornings in your mad dash to get out the door.)
- You need to believe that you have the ability to do it. (In essence, you are capable and worthy.)
- You must have a trigger in place to help you do it. (For many people this might be an alarm clock, or leaving the mini-blinds in your bedroom adjusted so the light of the rising sun awakens you.)

I am a fan of Fogg's work but I have developed my own set of four core requirements that I have come to see as vital for people who are attempting to thrive or sustain a thriving way of life in a high-demand job or work culture.

Figure 8.1 shows the Core Four.

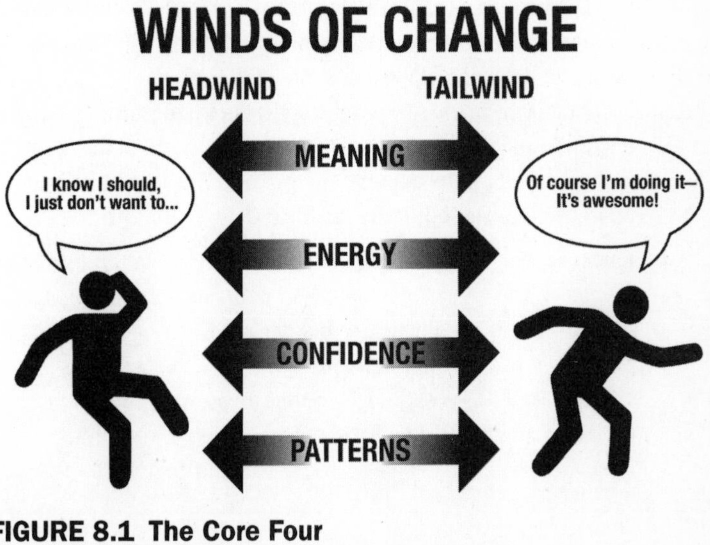

FIGURE 8.1 The Core Four

The Core Four

1. **Meaning.** You must have a reason underlying what you choose to do, and especially as you seek to make changes. There must be a clear and meaningful WHY that you could recite on cue.

2. **Confidence.** You must believe you can behave as you desire, or that you can learn to make the change(s).

3. **Energy.** You must have sufficient physical and emotional energy to undertake and sustain an activity or change.

   Let me say two things about energy here. (There's more later in the book.) First, as you perceive the way you want to structure or strategize a "good day," you are likely to put too many good tasks into that day *initially*. You will be wise to limit yourself to just the few tasks or even a singular behavior that are essential, in line with your values, goals, and beliefs. The fewer the behaviors that you seek to build into your definition of a good day, the less energy you will need to get those behaviors molded into a pattern.

   Second, don't beat yourself up if you don't see yourself as having much energy. Your feelings of exhaustion, stress, of being out of balance, or of being "worn out" are likely what has led you to read this book! Energy will come increasingly as you work on motivation, confidence, and patterns.

   Sufficient to the day are the activities thereof! The factors and patterns described in the remaining chapters of this book are not designed to deplete energy or to exhaust all of your energy resources, but rather, to build energy.

4. **Patterns.** For lasting motivation and energy, it isn't sufficient to trigger the start of a behavior. You must establish *patterns* that consistently trigger the desired behaviors. Patterns help triggers and behaviors to become self-sustaining—or "self-fueling." B.J. Fogg advises that if you want to maximize behavior change, you should "put hot triggers in the path of motivated people." I agree and would add that if you want

those behaviors to become lasting, if not habitual, they need to be encased in daily patterns.

Would you like to see how you rate on the Core Four? Take the Thriver Quiz at www.andycore.com/quiz.

Keep in mind that every time you choose to do what you know you should do, you earn positive Behavioral Momentum and create a bit of positive energy that propels you forward. The flip side is also true—anytime you procrastinate, in essence negating or saying "no" to a behavior that you want to do or know you should do, you subtract from motivational energy.

The effects of your behavior accumulate—they add up! The more positive choices you make that turn into positive behaviors, the more you create the energy that is available and that prompts future action. That's how a *pattern* is built. It is the product of ongoing motivation, accumulated energy, and growing confidence.

Let's take a look at how this plays out.

What a Pattern Does for You

Julie and her husband were scheduled to leave for a vacation in Hawaii in two days. Julie, however, did *not* want to go. She said to me, "Andy, Hawaii is my favorite place to vacation. My husband and I need some time together. I knew we would likely have a very good time. But, I'm really in a good pattern right now. I've been doing things I know I should do on a daily basis. My work is going well, my health and exercise patterns are good, my attitude is good. I'm afraid that if I go on vacation right now, I'll lose the momentum I've built up. I don't want to revert to my old ways."

I encouraged her to see that she could maintain her new patterns, even in a different environment that had somewhat different tasks and activities.

Julie and I especially explored the ways in which a pattern had given her strength to stay motivated. Motivation, of course is momentum in disguise. I shared with her this Core Concept:

(continued)

(continued)

Core Concept: Think about it so you don't have to think about it.

In my presentations to some audiences, I show a series of five images that each have grey and black dots. The first image has many more grey dots than black, and then as the sequence progresses, the percentage of dots shifts so that the final image has many more black dots than gray. I ask, "In all five images taken together, are there more grey dots or black dots?" More than 90 percent of the people say there are more black dots.

In fact, there are more grey dots than black in the five images, but because the last image has so many black dots, a tendency called "recency bias" kicks in. The audience members are influenced by what they experienced "most recently."

When I show all five images simultaneously, rather than in a sequence, almost half of the group will guess correctly that there are more grey dots. Even so, the image with predominantly black dots that is perceived last in a sequence is a powerful cue that leads the other half of the audience to see black as the most dominant color across all five images.

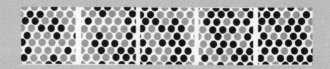

FIGURE 8.2 Recency Bias

Here's how the phenomenon plays out in a daily habitual pattern.

When a person has a good day filled with positive patterns and cues—a day in which the person does all those things he or she thinks he should do daily—that good day is held in memory as a highly positive incentive or trigger to *continue* or *replicate* the behavior of the previous day.

If a pattern has become entrenched to the point that it is *habitual*, this means that a person automatically responds according to the pattern in an instinctual way. The pattern has become ingrained, and will continue even if environmental or circumstantial factors change.

I asked Julie, "Do you believe you have developed new patterns that have become habits? Do you think that these patterns are almost instinctual—you do them almost without thinking about them?"

"Yes," she said.

"Then," I encouraged her, "go to Hawaii, Julie! Trust that the good patterns you've established will be continued there! Trust that even if they stray a bit, when you return home and restart your current daily way of life it will trigger your positive patterns to take up where you left off."

A Pattern Creates a Tailwind

One morning my wife, Naomi, was running late and she couldn't find her keys. She became almost frantic. She was late! The keys were missing!

At that point, our four-year-old daughter, Camille, said, "Momma, sit down." Naomi is a very patient person, and even in a rush she did what our daughter asked.

Camille then pulled Naomi's hair back and leaned in to look in her ear. She looked and looked, and finally Naomi said, "Honey, what are you doing?" Camille replied, "I don't know what is wrong. I've seen this done before and it worked."

What Camille had seen "done" before was the coin trick that parents have done for hundreds of years, where they "magically" pull a coin or some other small object from their ear. Camille was looking for magic—in her childlike thinking, she fully expected to be able to pull keys from her mother's ear!

(continued)

(*continued*)

The things we seek to build into our day *are* a little magical. A trigger that prompts an ingrained pattern can save us lots of time and hassle. Indeed, it can help create a tailwind for us that is both motivating and energy-producing.

Consider the fact that my wife, at that time, did not have a pattern for where she put her car keys when she entered the house. She might toss them in her purse, lay them on the kitchen desk, stick them in a tray on her dresser in the bedroom, or leave them in a coat pocket. Seconds, and sometimes frantic minutes, were spent every day *looking* for keys.

Once Naomi decided to adopt a new pattern—a change in how she dealt with her keys—things changed. She came to regard as the opening of the kitchen door as a "trigger" that prompted a set pattern of behavior: she kept her keys in her hand *until* she put the keys in a small decorative dish that was placed just a couple of steps from the door.

Simple.

But effective.

Not only did Naomi *always* know where her keys were, but I knew and so did the girls. The result was no more rushing, no more stress produced by rushing, no more confusion, and no more "I know I should but don't" twinges of self-incrimination.

Anytime a person falls short of meaning . . . or energy . . . or confidence . . . or experiences a failure of pattern, a headwind is generated. Life becomes just a little harder and a little more stressful.

On the other hand, when a person moves into a situation with great meaning, sufficient energy, and high confidence—and a pattern is in place that helps a person "act without thinking about acting"—there's a tailwind that makes life easier and less stressful.

If an alarm clock triggers you not only to get up, but also to lace on your walking shoes, and if lacing on your walking shoes becomes a second trigger that says, "Go out for a walk down to the park and back," then a pattern is being established that becomes instinctual to you. The resulting behavior gives you more confidence, more motivation, and more energy as you move through the rest of a morning. It sets you up for ongoing positive behaviors.

Carrying this one step further, the person finds it easier to do other "good for me" behaviors after that first set of good behaviors has been completed. It actually seems to take less effort and energy to do the right things as the day progresses.

A Lower Rate of Perceived Exertion

In the world of human performance research, the concept of "rate of perceived exertion" (RPE) is often measured to help a person see how much effort or energy that person *believes* he is using in order to do a task or manifest a particular behavior. For example, if a person is asked to run at a rate of six miles per hour on a treadmill for several minutes, and is asked how much energy the task is taking, they will say something like, "It feels like an eight out of a possible on the effort scale."

With that as a baseline, a coach, physiologist, or psychologist might give the person basic tools and physical and mental training. After only a few weeks of running, when the test is given again and the person is asked how it feels to run for several minutes at a six-mile-per-hour rate, the person is likely to say it felt like a "four" on the scale, perhaps even lower.

The result is that the body and mind have adapted to the new pattern and the person *perceives* that the activity takes significantly less effort.

The interesting aspect to this kind of study is that the change is not just in the person's physical strength and conditioning, but also, it is a change in their *perception*.

People who are Strivers and Strugglers very often feel as if they are facing an almost constant headwind in their lives. Often everything feels hard to them. They have a very high daily RPE. They feel as if they are continually bucking a trend, trying to overcome a hurdle, or are in a race against time that never stops. This state leaves them consistently asking, "Why don't I want to do what I know I should?"

(continued)

(*continued*)

Thrivers, on the other hand, are those who have established patterns that consistently fuel the Core Four and feel as if they are running with a tailwind. They feel calm, free, and energized instead of running into a headwind or as if they are in a straitjacket trying to get free.

If you are feeling oppressed in any way about your daily habits, take a long look at the Core Four I described earlier:

- Are you truly motivated to act in a positive way—do you have a good reason for doing what you do? Are you seeking to make changes in your day that are for a good purpose, aimed at a good goal? Are these positive reasons and purpose clear to you?

- Are you fueling your body with the right things for physical and emotional energy? Do you have enough stamina to do what you are hoping to do in the new pattern for your day?

- Are you confident that you can do what you need to do or feel you should do? Or are you reasonably confident you can learn what to do?

- Are you going through the course of your new "patterns" in a way that is engraving a pattern into your mind? Are you using triggers to create patterns that can give you a tailwind?

If you feel that life has a very high RPE, one or more of these four elements is either missing or is out of whack. Isolate which one(s).

Have you seen the movie *Jaws*? It was my father's favorite movie and every time he concluded that there was nothing good to watch on television, out came the VHS of *Jaws*. I have seen that movie more often than any other!

If you have not seen it, *Jaws* is the story of a gigantic shark that eats people. I could probably recite the dialogue word for word, but let me focus on my favorite part in the movie. Quinn, the salty, angry, grizzled shark hunter finds Jaws out in the middle of the ocean.

The way Quinn hunts and captures sharks is by shooting them with a harpoon that has a rope attached to a big plastic barrel filled with pressurized air. The barrel is hard to sink, and the more the shark attempts to run or dive deep with the buoyant barrel in tow, the more energy the shark exerts. Eventually, the shark wears out and becomes easy prey for Quinn.

Most sharks Quinn has encountered aren't strong enough to pull more than one or two barrels under water, but Jaws does this easily. So Quinn and his crew shoot a third harpoon tied to a third barrel of pressurized air. To their amazement, Jaws is also able to pull three barrels underwater. They shoot again—a harpoon attached to an unheard-of fourth barrel! Jaws takes the fourth barrel underwater, but not for long. Eventually, this much resistance is too much even for a supersized monster.

Think of yourself as Quinn. The Core Four concepts of Motivation, Energy, Confidence, and Patterns are the harpoons and barrels. No bad habit, lack of willpower or self-doubt can last if your day is consistently fueling the Core Four. Stick these barrels into your day and you will sink your fluctuating willpower, focus, and energy issues and you will rise to greater success.

When all four barrels are in full force and you are experiencing a true tailwind to your day, you are likely going to find it easy to:

- Pick up the phone and make the call . . . that one that you previously found so hard to make after the blahs hit in the middle of the afternoon.

- Reach for a healthy "raw food" snack rather than a cookie . . . which you previously would never have done when you felt the need for something to munch.

- Dash off a quick thank-you e-mail rather than give in to a round of e-reader Solitaire . . . which is what you might have chosen as a means of overcoming boredom or work fatigue.

- Pick up the papers scattered across your desk and sort, file, or toss them before leaving the office . . . which formerly seemed like something difficult at the end of a 10-hour workday.

(continued)

(*continued*)

None of the tasks or decisions described above are major, or take extraordinary energy or amounts of time. But tasks as simple as making a call, writing a quick note, organizing a pile of paper, or making a healthy food choice can seem very difficult to a person who is bucking a headwind.

The fact for most people in the above examples is that the task—the call, the note, the paper sort, the snack—is going to have to be done eventually, and when that time comes, it will be more resented and seem to take longer than the few seconds involved. You will finish the task and think, "Why did I wait on this?" Remember, the feeling of "Why don't I want to do what I know I should?" is often a sign that you are walking into a motivation headwind. Why put yourself through that? Why set yourself up for an oppressive burdensome *feeling* that life is harder than it really is?

Ultimately, it is so much easier to Change Your Day and establish patterns that energize you fully and keep you motivated all the way to bedtime. It is so much easier to feed your mind the right motivational messages, fuel your body and emotions with the right nutrients, bolster your confidence with small accomplishments, and live out instinctual habits of simply "doing the right things" (right, of course, being what you have determined) than to hurl yourself into a day relying on willpower and *hoping* that somehow the pieces are going to automatically fall into place for you like the right color balls into the roulette wheel.

To Change Your Day . . .

Remember:

- The changes that build momentum are rooted in decisions, not additional tasks.
- The building of a pattern does not require you to make a list of things to add to your daily schedule.

In most instances, you will simply be adjusting what you are already doing, or want to do, in a way that becomes more habitual.

- Thrivers' daily way of life fuels the Core Four and creates a motivational tailwind.

Now is the time to ask yourself:

1. Do I have a strong reason for *wanting* to do certain things in my day? Do the things that I think I *should* do have value and good purpose?

2. Do I have a base of energy for doing what I want to do in a day? If the answer is "maybe not," pare down what you want to do in a day so you can feel more accomplished and fueled by the momentum you build.

3. Do I feel confident that I can do—or I can *learn* to do—what I want to do in a given day?

4. Am I willing to develop triggers that produce patterns?

If the answer is "yes" to these four sets of questions . . . you're ready to launch.

CHAPTER 9

Breaking Down the Change Process

When I was in graduate school, I was broke. Not a little short but downright broke! Many days I scrounged under the cushions in my couch to try to come up with 79 cents to buy a bean burrito for lunch.

Then one day a friend told me that he was making money as a substitute teacher. The light came on: "Easy money!"

On my first day as a substitute teacher, an elementary school principal assigned me to a physical education class. I thought it was nice of the principal to give me an easy assignment on my first day out. Little did I know she was feeding me to the lions.

The first thing an elementary PE teacher must do is have the students sit in a row on the baseline of a gym floor. As a group of kindergartners burst into the gym, I looked into one child's eyes and saw the odd combination of happiness and desperation that I had come to associate with someone who had been up all night drinking Turkish coffee.

I asked the students, in a calm and inviting tone, to sit on the baseline. I even added "Please." They not only ignored me, but began to run around the gym in a faster and more chaotic pattern. I added a little volume: "Okay, okay, I need everyone to sit on the line." Nothing happened. Finally, I yelled, "On the line, *now!*" Two sweet little girls sat down on the line, but the other 21 children organized themselves to run in a circle around me, laughing as they ran.

I'll spare you the next 10 minutes of my frustration. The only thing that seemed to work was when I picked out one child, caught him and sat him down on the line and watched for a few seconds to ensure he did not get up. Then I grabbed another child, sat her down, and waited to ensure she stayed put, checked on the previous child, and then grabbed a third child. I didn't know what else to do, so I grabbed a fourth child, determined to get all 23 children seated on the line even if it took the full 30 minutes of gym class.

And then something interesting happened around the fifth child. It was as if chaos noticed a pattern developing. I kid you not, the rest of the children started sitting down on their own!

It took me 10 minutes to get the first three students seated. All the while, a vein seemed about ready to burst in my head from high blood pressure. But then, it only took three minutes to get the rest of the class organized. Not only did the feeling of pressure leave my brain, but I *smiled*! I was motivated and energized to finish the time period with a rousing activity the children loved!

I went home from that first day of substitute teaching absolutely exhausted. I was so tired I did something I have never done before or since—I feel asleep while sitting at a stoplight.

I also learned two great lessons that day:

One, I learned that if I could conquer the chaos generated by a group of kindergartners, I could conquer any other type of chaos that might emerge in my life!

Two, I learned that to get control of both chaos and complexity, the key is to focus on one thing at a time.

One child at a time.

One behavior at a time.

And one day at a time!

Core Concept: Pick One

Resist the urge to change your whole life. Pick one change you desire for your day. Make it a realistic goal. And then pursue it until you tackle it and hold it down.

Don't take on more than you can tackle and hold down!

Too many changes are counterproductive. Take on what you can take on. And then add a change only as you are *ready* to add *one*!

FOCUS ON JUST ONE CHANGE

The number one New Year's resolution across decades and across the United States is "lose weight." People think this is a singular change. It is not.

To lose weight a person will likely need to eat healthier, eat smaller quantities, and become more physically active. That's three changes, not one.

Focus on one of the three. If you choose "eat healthier," you are still facing a change that has multiple facets. Eating healthier doesn't mean eating more lettuce and less grease. That may be one part of eating healthier, but a healthier eating pattern is likely to have many facets to is, such as:

- Drink more pure water and less of other beverages.
- Eat five to six small meals a day and make sure to have a bit of protein at each one.
- Eliminate most refined sugars, which can be found in processed foods, iced tea, and even salad dressings. Know the many terms for sugar that appear on processed-food labels.
- Don't buy products with trans fats or partially hydrogenated fats listed among the ingredients.
- Read labels.
- Eat five servings of fresh fruits a day.
- Eat five servings of vegetables a day.

The list goes on. Even in reading these seven specific aspects of "healthier" eating, you may feel yourself clenching. That's a lot of change! That's difficult!

After a few days you are likely to conclude, "This is too hard," and revert back to whatever "old" eating habits you have had in place for years, even decades.

Consider, instead, what might happen if a person sets a New Year's resolution of "drink a full glass of ice water every time I feel hungry." This is easy to do because you have a trigger and a positive pattern.

Trigger: You feel hungry.
Pattern: Drink a glass of cold water.

This trigger/pattern approach to change is very effective. It capitalizes on simplicity, cues and behavioral momentum, gives a sense of accomplishment and increasing confidence, and can easily be connected to more meaningful changes; for example, this behavior makes it a lot easier to drink enough water to be healthier and maintain higher energy.

One change.

But, oh, the difference that change CAN make!

What if the change is, "Drink water *only*."

One change.

But that one change represents many changes in your health management. Drinking only water means eliminating fruit juices and sugar-laced sodas and other beverages, which can mean a significant decrease in total calorie count and a corresponding decrease in weight.

If you decide your New Year's health resolution is going to be to "exercise more," there are also numerous subchanges required for most people. Try one change: Wear walking shoes to work and carry dressier shoes in a tote bag.

This one change will encourage you to do more walking around your office, to go out for a walk at noon, and perhaps even substitute part of a lunch hour for a walk.

Trigger: It's lunch time.
Pattern: Go for a walk.

Or consider this one change: Arrange to walk or cycle all or part of your way to work on Fridays. That one change has multiple benefits.

Trigger: It's Friday.
Pattern: Ride my bike to work.

I am not negating the benefit of having a big goal. I also am not negating the value of defining the ultimate outcome you want to achieve. What I am saying is that for you to implement a change that works on a daily basis, you need to break that big goal down and choose a piece that can be accomplished in a day. You need to be able to fit a goal into a daily pattern or minipattern that is workable and motivating at the *daily* level.

There is a tremendous benefit in breaking down goals. Doing this makes a day seem less complex, and in checking off the accomplishment of even a very small goal, you will experience a motivating, energizing effect. Your confidence will grow! Above all, you will feel more in control of your own goals, your own time, your own impulses, and your own progress. Control is vital to the entire process of personal change.

One task at a time.

One change at a time.

One *portion* of work at a time.

These are small changes that fall readily into a daily schedule.

I once provided research for a PBS affiliate in Arkansas on a program titled *Fighting Fat*. I was cohost for the show and my job was to interview guests before a taping. The guests were overweight people having trouble with losing weight. One guest, who was 75 pounds overweight, said, "Andy, I really don't eat that much." I dug deeper and discovered that what she *really* meant was that she didn't eat that often. She would skip meals during the day—proudly eating "only two meals a day"—but she had her second meal at night, right before going to bed, and she consumed a massive amount of calories at that meal. That's a sure way to gain fat as fast as humanly possible!

She not only needed to graze her way through six small meals a day, but make sure those small meals were truly small!

Often a task or goal has been broken down into something of a bite-sized piece, but is not given sufficient time for the chewing and digesting of even that small task. In setting up a sequence of changes, make sure that small tasks are given sufficient time, and that whenever possible, a string of small tasks are sequenced so you can build some momentum in doing them.

Anticipate the Stages of Change

There seem to be several stages for all types of change, including changing your day. If you are aware of them at the outset, you are likely to be able to persevere through them.

Stage One

Make a quality decision to change.

Put emphasis on the word *quality*. Change should never be approached casually or half-heartedly. If a change is important to make, it should be given the mental importance it deserves. Committing to a new change is fast and often too easy. Being committed is a different story. The time required for stage one: usually less than a minute.

Stage Two

You begin to make the change and feel clunky and awkward. You face resistance, usually not from yourself alone, but sometimes from others. The thought of "quitting" buzzes around your head like a fly, taunting, "This isn't going to work!" At times, that fly seems to sail into your mouth and you swallow it, choking and truly irritated. What to do? Spit out the fly and keep going.

At some point in this stage, unpredictable in time but predictable in that it *will* happen, you will begin to think *This might just work*. These positive thoughts tend to increase in intensity and frequency. At that point, you feel a determination to endure, to continue with whatever effort is required.

The time required for stage two: usually between three days and three weeks.

Stage Three

You keep plugging away, and much of the time, you feel strong motivation and confidence related to your path and your progress. Interruptions can still occur, and they can be highly disruptive, but if you work through the interruptions and return to the pattern you are establishing, you can and *will* grow stronger in your resolve and in your execution of the pattern. The time required for stage three: three days to three months.

Did you ever watch an episode of a television show called *Supernanny*? Jo, a trained nanny, takes the most obnoxious children and turns them into models of self-discipline. How did she do this? In essence, she helped the parents and children Change Their Day by creating a consistent daily schedule and made them stick with it until it stuck!

When these children were first forced to abide by Jo's rules and schedule, they acted like wild stallions put into a fenced area. They bashed against the walls, yelled, leaped about in pure rage, and threw terrible tantrums. But, after a while, the rules and structure gave them a sense of comfort, so much so that they willingly kept the rules and schedule, and even grew to *want* the rules and schedule to stay in place.

Be aware that the new changes you are seeking to implement in your day may be confining and demanding at first. Your old habits may rear up like wild stallions. Stick with your plan. Keep at it. Be firm with yourself. You'll find it easier as you stay consistent—to the point where you truly come to *enjoy* the process and take great joy in the rewards!

Stage Four

In this stage you become consistent enough in your pattern that you start finding ways to integrate and adapt your new change to other segments of your day and other areas of your life as a whole. You willingly are doing what you believe you *should* do, and you become strong in countering those who try to stop you or discourage you from living out your new change. Psychologists call this phase "orgasmic integration"—and yes, it does feel good! Maybe not *that* good, but still really good. The good news is that you can experience it in public without getting arrested. The time required to experience stage four: three weeks to 66 days.

The commonly held belief that it takes "21 days to form a habit" has come under fire from researchers recently. The new estimate is closer to 66 days. This could be discouraging, but let me let you in on a little secret. You can't get to 66 days without getting through this day. Getting through today with positive momentum leads to tomorrow being a bit better, and soon you'll look up and it's past 66 days and you are miles down the road toward your goal with the winds of change at your back, thinking, *Of course I'm doing this, it feels awesome!*

Even so, I think the 21- or 66-day estimates are a bit misleading. Sure, full integration happens pretty far down the path, but I've seen people achieve or recapture a highly motivated and optimistic state as quickly as in 10 days, and sometimes even faster. It just might take a bit longer for it to be "orgasmic."

Of course, it depends on the action you are implementing and how strong the triggers are. I've seen exercise, when done right, swing someone's motivation to where their "want" increased significantly in as few as three days. I worked with one client who was having trouble "leaving work at work," and was often thinking of her work during her personal time and it was making her more anxious and less "present" with her significant other. I helped her build a habit of "journaling" into her day. We worked through the basic way to journal and the time that might be optimal for her to journal during a given day. Her trigger was 5 PM. The pattern was to pull out her journal and outline her top three tasks for tomorrow. She was surprised at how effective this was at helping her leave her worry about work at work. After one day, she was hooked and felt highly motivated to journal the next day. She is still journaling daily after eight and a half years. It is such a built-in part of her day that she no longer even puts it on a list of things to do. It is as natural to her as brushing her teeth or putting on lipstick in the morning. I've seen people learn to love Brussels sprouts in . . . well, I've never met anyone who learned to "love" Brussels sprouts. Tolerate, perhaps. Those things are nasty.

The point is that many people who are making changes in their day find that they feel motivated after only a few days of initiating a new pattern in their life. Remember, motivation is an experiential lesson.

Full integration of a change may take several weeks, but I've seen some people gain or recapture a high level of motivation and optimism in as little as three days, and I've seen a few people change even faster.

The degree to which you progress to high motivation and high energy is going to depend upon the nature of the change you are seeking to implement, the number of changes you are seeking to put into a new pattern in a day, and the strength of the triggers that initiate change behaviors.

Two caveats are worth highlighting:

1. Most of the time, a person doesn't move through these four stages in a smooth, tight, time-predictable, or linear fashion. Change of any type is a bit messier than some researchers want to admit. You may jump back and forth between two stages, or skip a stage entirely. If that happens, it's okay.

2. No matter what you choose to change, you will find that the most important day in the change process is today. Stay focused in the day and face tomorrow . . . tomorrow.

To Change Your Day . . .

Pick one thing you want to change . . . *just one thing* . . . and chase that change until you have fully integrated it into your life.

CHAPTER 10

Checklists and Big-Box Management

For both of our best interests, I always interviewed potential clients before we agreed to work together. I started with what I call my five "Lip Service" questions. If they said no to any of these five questions, I knew that the person was not serious about making changes and just giving lip service to the notion. In my mind, the most important of those questions is, "Are you willing to write down your goals as a checklist?"

KEEP THE FLYING FORTRESS IN THE AIR

I first read about the Flying Fortress in Atul Gawande's excellent book *The Checklists Manifesto*. I have been fascinated by this famous war plane ever since.

The Army had asked Boeing to produce a bomber that was faster, could fly farther, and could carry more bombs than anything in the Army's fleet at the time. Boeing overdelivered. The plane it produced could carry five times the bombs the Army requested, and it could fly farther and faster than expected.

The plane was set to debut at a military aircraft competition. With a great deal of fanfare, the plane took to the runway, roared into action, and lifted off with ease. It climbed upward—100 feet, 200 feet, and then, at 300 feet, all smiles turned into expressions of astonishment and horror as the plane stalled and then plummeted to the ground and exploded.

Some of the most talented and renowned pilots in the military had been chosen to fly the plane on that day. When the investigation was concluded regarding the cause of the crash, the report read "pilot error."

In 1939, very little was automated in aircraft. A pilot had to manage four engines, landing gear, and a great many other systems—manually and simultaneously. In this case, the pilot had missed one simple detail, and that detail turned out to be critical!

The Flying Fortress was thought to be too complex for one pilot to handle. Full production on the plane was put on hold. The Army bought a few planes as "test planes," and got busy trying to figure out how to avoid crashes of this plane in the future.

Let me challenge you. If you were put in charge of figuring out how to fly a very complex aircraft, what approach would you take for training pilots? Common sense might dictate that you choose a pilot and have him specialize in that plane, and then provide extensive, time-consuming, and expensive training that would enable him to "think on his feet" and handle a wide variety of complex details "in the moment." In other words, learn the operational manual and rehearse, rehearse, rehearse.

This approach is frequently used in business. Some corporate training manuals are so big they would choke a wood chipper.

The Army, however, did not choose this approach. Instead of providing mountains of information and months of training, they worked with a group of pilots to create a short, sequenced checklist for flying the plane.

The pilots knew what to do, and they knew the steps necessary to prepare, take off, fly, and land the plane. They knew *how* to do each step. The need was for the steps to be put into sequence as a *checklist*.

The checklists were reduced to a series of index cards.

Remember that most airplanes up to 1939 were fairly simple machines to fly. The Flying Fortress was more *complex* than other plane of its era, and it was, therefore, too complex for "winging it" with gut instincts. The complexity had to be made simple, and the solution was a sequence of steps that could be "checked off" for each flight.

From the day the checklist was completed, tested, double-checked, and approved, the Flying Fortress flew more than 1.8 million miles without a single accident, and it turned out to be one of the decisive advantages of the Allied Forces in defeating the Nazis in World War II.

MAKING THE COMPLEX SIMPLE

In my work, I have the opportunity to learn the job roles of a wide variety of professions. I am often amazed at how complex many work situations and production processes are. They boggle the average mind. The amount of information that must be managed, the multiple responsibilities that must be juggled, and the high volume of decisions that must be made can and often do add up to an overwhelming tide that swamps willpower, the ability to concentrate, and, most of all, the ability to make reliable, high-quality decisions.

Simple checklists can help tremendously. They can ensure that important tasks are not forgotten and are completed in a timely, sequential, and foolproof manner. A checklist also keeps you from having to remember every detail, which also frees up tremendous quantities of "mental energy" that can be aimed at creative tasks, improved efficiency, quality control or quality improvement, and streamlined processes.

Anytime a checklist can be shortened, without a breakdown in a system or a "crash," all the better! The key at that point is to make sure no vital step is eliminated from the list, and that all things that need to be in sequence remain in sequence.

Thrivers use checklists better and more often than Strivers.

NEVER A SIGN OF WEAKNESS

I have encountered people who regard a checklist—or any type of "systematic operating procedure"—as a form of personal weakness. They *want* to see themselves as strong or smart to the point that they don't *need* a written checklist. The exact opposite is true, in my opinion. If you're going to fly a complex airplane or fly a complex life, you are wise to use checklists!

Here are three practical insights into checklists:

1. The more practical the items on the list, the easier they are to "schedule." And the more practice you gain in practical behaviors, the better and faster you tend to become at completing them.

2. You should not need to define what you put on a checklist beyond the words on the list. For example, don't write, "Take time to smell the roses."

   What does that item *mean*? If you actually have a rose garden with fragrant varieties, fine, then do add this. But if this means sitting on a park bench and watching children play for 15 minutes . . . or working in your garden for a half hour after work . . . or practicing your photography skills . . . then put down "park," "garden," or "photo time."

3. How often you consult a checklist is up to you. The same goes for the information you put on a checklist. I certainly don't advocate that a person turn off the alarm clock in the morning and pull out an index card with a checklist on it. A checklist is generally useful until a person has fully integrated the things on the list into daily life, to the point that the behaviors become instinctual.

GOING FROM TO-DO TO DONE

For years I made to-do lists—long, detailed lists of things that were fairly mundane and also extremely profound.

The truth is, I rarely got to the end of any one list before I started over with a new list. I know I'm not alone in this. From time to time, I'd get frustrated with myself because I tended to put the most important things at the bottom of my list and work off the list sequentially . . . which meant that the most important things were never addressed! I often got stuck completing the urgent rather than the important.

I found a simple solution. I put a box in front of each item on my list. For the less important items I made the box *small*. For the important items, I made the box *big*.

This isn't rocket science and it isn't tremendously profound. But it worked for me. And I've seen it work for hundreds of other people. I call my checklist system "Big-Box Time Management" (see Figure 10.1).

Those things that are more important get a bigger box, and when the task is completed, it gets a whopping big checkmark.

At the end of the day, if the big boxes have big checkmarks, that day is generally a "good day" in my book. If I could get a

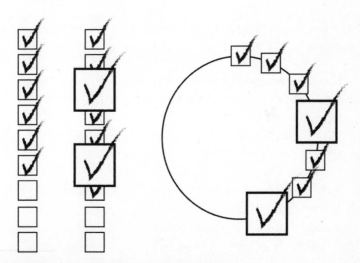

FIGURE 10.1 Big-Box Time Management

lot of little boxes checked off, great. But I didn't focus on the little-box tasks. I focused on the Big Boxes.

Doing this has made me feel far more satisfied, relaxed, and accomplished at the end of most days, in comparison to the way I felt when recopying my endless stream of to-do lists.

BIG-BOX MANAGEMENT

Big-Box Management is the foremost way I know to keep goals at the forefront of your daily patterns and the changes you are chasing. It is a way to both manage your time to get more accomplished, and also to simplify choice-making.

The Big-Box approach calls upon a person to identify the things that must be done for the person to conclude that a day has been a "good day." It asks a person first to identify, "What do I value most?"

Let me share my own Big-Box profile with you.

I greatly value these things:

- Being as productive in my work as I can be.
- Having maximum positive physical energy.
- Having high-quality relationships with my wife and my daughters.

Then, for whatever values a person sets, Big-Box Management asks the person to write down specific questions related to each value.

The following are the Big-Box questions that I ask myself.

1. If I have only two hours to work today, what must I do to be the most productive I can be?
   - *Did I write?* Writing is the backbone of my creative work. It might be research and writing for a live presentation, or research and writing for a book.

- *Did I reach out to someone who might benefit from my services or can help me promote my services?* Specifically, did I make calls to offer my speaking services? Did I communicate with a publisher or editor of my material? Did I set an appointment with someone who might refer me to an outlet for the information and inspiration I can give to an audience?

  I like what Larry Winget, Pitbull of Personal Development, has said about work success: "If you are not as successful as you want; it is either that your product sucks or you are not asking enough people to buy it." I don't want to be guilty of either! I want my writing to be the best it can be, and I want to reach as many people as I can with the hope-filled, practical messages I desire to convey!

2. What will help me have maximum positive physical energy? My questions are:
   - *Did I exercise?* I know that if I fail to do this almost daily, I am not nearly as positive in my attitude, or as productive in my work. Physical exercise is an energizer, not an energy depleter. I know this from both personal experience and a mountain of research studies.

3. What specific things might I do in a day to build an even stronger and more vibrant relationship with my two daughters and my wife?
   - *Did I play?* Emotional energy is directly related to "having fun." One of the things I love most is Daddy-Daughter date night.

     On date night, five-year-old Camille and I usually head for the Green Submarine, her favorite restaurant, and then we go to a movie, and after the movie, get ice cream.

     I enjoy this time thoroughly, but if you ask Camille if this is the most favorite thing she does with Daddy, she'll very honestly tell you, "No." Her most fun thing is "when we play on the trampoline," or "play monster at the park."

I'm not ashamed to admit that I spend a lot of evenings on our trampoline, and also getting my nails painted and playing the "monster" in a game that involves my girls being magical princesses that can always defeat a monster and turn it into a good person. (Think *Beauty and the Beast*!)

I strongly encourage you, if you do NOT have a child in your life with whom you can play regularly, to find one!

- *Did I share?* Of all the things I might do to make my wife Naomi feel loved, the one thing she appreciates most is when we spend quality time together. She knows I am being "fully present" as she speaks, and for her, that is translated into "sharing." She perceives that I am truly sharing myself as I listen closely to her tell about her world, her concerns, her opportunities or challenges, or even the Facebook updates she found interesting. By her definition, sharing is easy!

AT THE END OF THE DAY . . .

Given the information I just provided above, here is how my Big-Box set of questions is summarized for any given day:

- Did I write/create?
- Did I attempt to extend my influence and services?
- Did I exercise?
- Did I play with my daughters?
- Did I share quality time with my wife?

I've had these same Big Boxes for long enough that I don't have to pull out an index card or my journal. Right before I go to sleep at night, I can check through this set of questions mentally, and if I can check off a "yes" to each of these questions . . . then it was a good day!

I have a strong sense that the day had purpose (and that it reinforced my personal set of values), it had joy, and it was "complete" in helping me fulfill my long-term goals. I think this state of mind is as powerful as any sleep aid in helping you drift off to deep, enjoyable sleep.

BIG BOXES ON A CLOCK FACE

Once I realized that my Big-Box activities tended to fall rather consistently at certain times of the day, I began to turn my previously linear lists into circular lists, somewhat like the face of a clock. That made my list more fun, and over time it also helped me isolate whether I seemed to be having a little difficulty getting certain tasks—or certain categories of tasks—done at a particular time of day. It also helped me isolate periods in my day when "interruptions" were more likely to occur, and to occur in a way that had an overall impact on my motivation or momentum.

Does a checklist *need* to be sequential through the hours of a day?

That is totally up to you.

As I already stated, one of my Big-Box items is to exercise daily. I find it easier to exercise early in my day, so I usually put that Big Box near the top of my list. My clients are located in the United States, Asia, and Europe, so making phone calls related to my business is usually most efficient after lunch or early evening when I can access more time zones more readily. It gets a Big Box midway through my list. Between exercise and phone calls is usually work. And toward the end of the day are times with my girls and my wife.

This does not mean at all that I value time with Bella, Camille, and Naomi any less. The Big Box that addresses my relationship with them is usually accomplished toward the end of a day.

A MEANS OF MANAGING INTERRUPTIONS

Big-Box Time Management in an "around-the-clock" format has helped me manage interruptions in a way that has greatly increased my productivity.

Let me give you a couple of examples.

At one point in my life, I seemed to "live" on my e-mail. Frequent e-mail interruptions dealt a serious blow to my creativity and productivity!

I came to a conclusion that I didn't need to read or answer every e-message in a matter of seconds. Most of them could wait until a designated hour later in the day.

In a Hewlett Packard commissioned survey by TNS Research, frequent interruptions by e-mail and text messages and phone calls showed a drop in IQ similar to losing an entire night's sleep or two and a half times greater than the drop in IQ caused by smoking marijuana. Who would have guessed! Even though this is not a double blind, peer-reviewed study, it is interesting how interruptions can affect your ability to concentrate, which is a necessity for most creative or detailed work.

Another study done in 2013 and published by the *International Journal of Stress Management* showed that frequent work interruptions were more costly to a company than just a decrease in productivity.* Don't interrupt me!

---

*Lin, Bing C., Kain, Jason M., Fritz, Charlotte, *International Journal of Stress Management, Vol 20(2)*, May 2013, 77–94. doi: 10.1037/a0031637

An examination of the relationship between intrusions at work and employees can become strained.

It seemed likely to me that the increase in interruptions actually *caused* a decrease in productivity. Specifically, however, the study showed that frequent interruptions in a person's work-flow increased exhaustion, anxiety, and physical ailments. Obviously the more exhausted, anxious, and physically uncomfortable a person becomes, the less that person is going to produce, and assuredly, the less he or she will produce in an efficient, high-quality manner.

A DIFFERENT KIND OF LIST TO "CHECK"

If you and I were sitting across from each other having coffee or tea, and we had only a few minutes to determine what is keeping you from being a full-fledged Thriver, or if you were asking yourself, "Why don't I want to do what I know I should?," these are the six questions I would ask you:

1. Can you articulate why you are working so hard? (In other words, what motivates you to put out all the energy and effort you exert? What is your reason?)
2. What is your mental reaction to the stress or frustration that you may feel as you face a "super-big" goal? (What is your response to a steep learning curve or a need to gain control over a process, procedure, or task?)
3. Do your daily patterns motivate you? (Do they build confidence in you that you are on an upward path to greater success?)
4. Do you have as much energy as you'd like to have, or need, to complete the tasks in any given day?
5. Do your daily patterns serve your core values?
6. Do you often feel a strong connection with others, or do you feel that you are "going it alone"?

To Change Your Day . . .

Remember:

- Make a Big-Box checklist associated with the important tasks you do at work.

- Answer the six questions at the end of this chapter. Give them some reflection.

- Decide where you need to jump in and make a change in your day.

CHAPTER 11

Triggers and Patterns

Triggers and Patterns

As much as 95 percent of what people do in a day is habitual, and much of that behavior follows a pattern or routine. Patterns exist and become fairly predictable to an objective observer whether the person is leading others, engaged in creative work, connecting with customers, meeting with coworkers, pursuing a health regimen, socializing with friends, or interacting with family members. You may not be nearly as aware of the patterns of your life as others are!

In many cases, a person's day does not have one overall predictable pattern, but rather, a series of mini-patterns. These include habitual ways of thinking (making decisions and choices) and behaving related to specific tasks and for limited periods of time.

For example, you likely have a predictable pattern every time you hear a phone ring, and especially if it is *your* phone. When a smartphone buzzes in your pocket, that becomes a trigger for you to check your phone and respond to the message it conveys to you. It also, of course, triggers others around you to check *their* phones!

Trigger: The ringing phone.

Pattern: You check your phone.

In some cases, a trigger reminds you to think of a particular person you love, or refocuses you on something that supports your values.

Some triggers are biological—a hunger pang or a sudden thirst can signal that it is time to eat or drink.

Most "chores" have a pattern. The trigger is the *need*—to get dressed for the day, to go grocery shopping, to pay bills, and so forth.

In some cases, however, a trigger can be an interruption in the flow of your day, and at times, a trigger can actually stop positive momentum.

A TWOFOLD CHALLENGE

In seeking to make a change in your day, you face a twofold challenge. The first is in recognizing the triggers and defining the pattern of behavior desired. Habits can develop spontaneously and subconsciously. A change in habits takes intention.

I like what Mark Twain once said: "Habit is habit, and not to be flung out of the window by any man, but coaxed downstairs a step at a time."

It may take a little introspection on your part to recognize triggers that have become automatic in your daily life. It most certainly will take reflection to determine what patterns follow triggers, and how you need to alter those patterns for a "change goal" to be accomplished!

The second challenge is practice. Once a person has isolated a pattern of change that needs adjusting, the response is to practice the new pattern . . . and continue to practice the new pattern until it completely overtakes and replaces an old pattern.

THE BY-PRODUCTS OF PRACTICE

My father was born with almost freakish eye-hand coordination. My grandmother and aunts love to tell the story of how my father had a "typing race" with his ninth-grade teacher in an "Introduction to Typing" class. The competition was set up in front of the entire class and the goal was to see who could type the most words in a given amount of time.

My father won the competition, beating the teacher by six words. Dad, however, was always quick to add that he also made three more mistakes than the teacher and, therefore, he believed the teacher had won. Regardless, it was a pretty amazing feat for a ninth grader to enter the class having never typed and to be able to type as fast as the typing teacher by the end of one semester.

I was not born with that same degree of eye-hand coordination. Typing was a difficult and complex skill for me to acquire. I was a "hunt and peck" typist all the way through college. Typing was a pain.

When I arrived at the University of Arkansas graduate school and faced the high volume of research papers that I was expected to produce, I quickly determined that my typing skills were not adequate! I knew that I *had* to improve my typing and improve it quickly or I'd never complete the workload ahead of me.

So, I bought a book and *relearned* how to type. At first, the new method felt awkward and I was frustrated that it consumed so much of my mental focus. I felt that I was actually typing slower than before. I became so irritated that I quit several times, and went back to the hunt-and-peck method. Then, it always seemed that I'd find myself sitting next to someone who could type with both hands, and when I saw how much faster they were at finishing a typing task, I'd try the new method again.

Finally, I *really* tried—nothing half-hearted about my effort! In less than three weeks I was typing full-hand and faster than ever. In the following months I kept getting faster and faster. I still would not want to challenge my father in typing, but I became very pleased with my speed.

And do you know what is even more satisfying than typing fast? It is putting my hands on the keyboard and without having to *think* about typing, the words just seem to appear on my computer screen. The complex skill that once required my full concentration and a big load of mental energy has now become almost instinctual. I type almost effortlessly, and in the process I discover that I love to type because I love to write. The writing and the typing have become one and the same.

This is the way patterns are intended to work in our lives.

Learning a new pattern takes effort and can be a bit tedious or laborious. But, once the new pattern has been learned—very often in three weeks or less—the new pattern actually "speeds" up performance and streamlines effort.

The pattern tends to produce more in less time. It makes a person more efficient, more productive, and along the way, allows the person to feel even more motivated and to have more "fun" in doing a task.

Your day is simply a series of mini-patterns. Remember, when you improve your daily patterns, you improve everything.

FOUR THINGS MINI-PATTERNS CAN DO FOR YOU

A mini-pattern is a sequence of a few steps done in response to a trigger. Most Thrivers eventually develop a series of mini-patterns that kick in throughout a day. Mini-patterns usually do not take a great deal of time—initially they may require some effort that translates into "learning time," but once they are learned mini-patterns usually save time.

The benefits of mini-patterns has been well-documented in behavioral research. Four main benefits seem to relate to all users!

Benefit 1: Clarity and Confidence

Mini-patterns that become second nature give a person clarity about *what* needs to be done—they usually give heightened awareness about "what comes next." Like the pilot's checklist of the Flying Fortress, these mini-patterns provide direction in an almost effortless way. The simultaneous byproduct is a high degree of confidence that the execution of the patterns will result in success.

Benefit 2: Less Decision-Making Stress

In a 2008 study published in the *Journal of Personality and Social Psychology*, researchers Kathleen D. Vohs, Roy F. Baumeister, and colleagues gave a group of participants a long list of choices to make. The second group was given a similar list to *consider*, but the participants were not asked to make any choices.

As part of the study, the participants were given a "cold presser task." This involved each person sticking his or her arm, to the elbow, into a container of ice and water that was circulated by an aquarium motor and kept at 0 degrees Celsius, or 32 degrees Fahrenheit. Participants first put their nondominant arm in room-temperature water for one minute to ensure an equal starting point. Then they put their dominant arm into the ice water and were instructed to hold it underwater for as long as possible.

Those who were "deliberators"—looking at a list to *consider*—were able to keep their arms in the ice bath for an average of 67 seconds before their willpower gave out.

The "deciders"—those being asked to make *choices*— gave up in less than half that time. They were only able to keep their arms in the ice water for an average of 27 seconds.

The researchers concluded that external factors directly impact decision-making ability. My contention is that internal stress always impacts decision-making. And furthermore, that a lowering of internal stress can help a person make clearer and better choices.

But there's one more conclusion I have drawn from this and other studies: People can lower their internal stress by making a few key choices *up front*, and allowing habitual patterns of behavior to kick in and help them reach choices and decisions faster and with greater positive impact.

I often hear from those I am coaching, "Andy, just tell me what do. If I have to make one more decision, I'll scream."

I'm not unsympathetic to their feelings. The magic of a mini-pattern is that once it is in place, you no longer have to decide what to decide! The pattern becomes the process. Do you remember the Core Concept in Chapter 8? Think about it so you don't have to think about it.

Core Concept: Think about it so you don't have to think about it.

The fewer the choices you have to make in a day about your day— and about task-related decisions—the lower your stress level, the greater your momentum, and the higher your achievement (productivity).

Benefit 3: Stronger Willpower

About every six months I become the person I aspire to help. Too many deadlines seem to converge with various other normal life processes, including, perhaps, too much travel and a member of my family becoming ill. My train is derailed. In a very short time I *can* go from functioning at peak performance to being a guy who stressed out, works too much, rarely exercises, and who is enjoying too many ales from my brother's brewery (www.corebeer.com). Pretty soon I realize I am more tired and crankier than normal, and I, too, find myself asking, "Why don't I do what I know I *should* do?"

It takes effort to sustain good patterns. But let me quickly move on to the good news: good patterns *help* willpower.

Willpower is a little like a "mental muscle" that must be trained and strengthened.

Researchers have shown that willpower is subject to the General Adaptation Syndrome theory. This theory simply states that if you stress something in the right way, you trigger improvement. We see this in physical exercise all the time—if a muscle is stressed correctly, it becomes stronger, faster, or has more endurance. In the case of willpower, if you "stress yourself" to add a new positive behavior to your line-up of daily mini-patterns, you not only have the motivational benefit of reaching your goals, but also, you strengthen the "mental muscle" that allows for change.

Willpower can be defined as a willingness and ability to do something that creates progress and, ideally, progress that is positive. When you challenge that willingness, and exert ability, willpower is enhanced.

The truth is you may not have all the willpower you need right now to sustain change, but you very likely have just enough willpower to *start* a change. If you will invest that willpower in Changing Your Day and actually DOing what you know you want to do, need to do, or should do on a daily basis, then the by-product of the DOing is greater results and growing willpower—enough to get up tomorrow and do, once again, the behavior associated with change. Over time and with repeated displays of willpower followed by activity, you learn how it *feels* to move toward your goals—you learn how greater focus, energy, and motivation are manifested. *Do-Know-*Be.

Willpower often emerges as almost a burst of energy.

Imagine that there is a large amount of willpower lying just behind a large iron door. To access the willpower, all you have to do is push open the door. This door, however, is really heavy. You begin to push and push, and finally you feel the door move just a *little*. That small result energizes you to keep pushing. There's a little more movement and that movement adds momentum to your efforts. It kind of feels like a tailwind. Again you feel energized to push more. And eventually the door begins to open faster until *suddenly*, the momentum swings the door open to reveal a wide new open expanse!

Benefit 4: Mini-patterns Trigger Increased Willpower and Sustained Motivation

Mini-patterns have a beginning and an ending. They take up a "unit of time." In doing so, they provide markers for giving yourself an "attaboy" or "way to go, girl" reward at the end of each mini-pattern. This is motivating and builds momentum, even if there are no signs of appreciation from other people.

Being a Navy SEAL is one of the most difficult jobs in the world, and the training to be a Navy SEAL is grueling. After three weeks of intensive mental and physical training, Hell Week arrives. It includes five and a half days of continuous training with only four hours of sleep . . . total. The candidate is pushed to extreme physical and mental limits in various conditions (such as having to frequently jump in info freezing California surf and lying still for an extended periods of time even when you are already freezing). The hypothermia, sleep deprivation, stress, and extreme fatigue result in more than two thirds of those who begin Hell Week to drop out.

One of the things that seems to allow candidates to succeed is a mind trick. During Hell Week, the Seals get four meals a day, rather than the standard three. This means a meal every six hours. Even in the throes of exhaustion and extreme stress, they keep their focus on, "Just make it to the next meal." They don't try to make it through the *week*, just the next six hours. One meal . . . and then another meal . . . and then another meal.

Think like a Navy SEAL.

Use mini-patterns to motivate you forward to the *next* thing on your daily checklist.

Set up rewards for the completion of each mini-pattern, even if it is just a big red X in a Big Box!

MINI-PATTERNS COMPEL ADDITIONAL CHANGES

Two Australian scientists—Megan Oaten, PhD, and Ken Cheng, PhD, at Macquarie University in Sydney—asked volunteers to focus on just one area of their life they wanted to change. After two months of diligently working at this change, they put the participants through a series of tests. They found that those who had stuck with their self-prescribed program tested better on self-control, had a greater ability to focus, and were better at ignoring distractions.

And there were even more "fringe" benefits. Even though they were not encouraged to make these changes, the subjects reported that their progress in making the one change led them to improve different areas of their life:

- Smoke less.
- Drink less alcohol.
- Eat less junk food and eat more healthful food.
- Monitor their spending more carefully.
- Procrastinate less and study more.
- Be more in control of their emotions.

Core Concept: One change usually fuels more changes.

What was the foremost activity these participants had pursued? Exercise.

The participants in the study had not been regular exercisers before the study. They also didn't go crazy in exercising—they averaged only one day of exercise a week in the first month of the study and only increased to an average of three times a week by the end of the second month. That's not a lot of exercise.

MINI-PATTERNS MAKE WAY FOR CREATIVE FLASHES

A final benefit of mini-patterns may not apply to *every person*, but I have seen mini-patterns enhance creativity in a high percentage of people.

I am an experienced driver and I live in an area that tends to have good roads, good road signs, and other citizens who are good drivers. The result is that I do not have to make an effort to drive unless there is a major thunderstorm or big construction projects on my normal driving routes. I'm not fully on autopilot, but on some days, it almost feels that way.

One of the byproducts of this for me is that some of my most creative ideas seem to come as I am driving.

This certainly wasn't the case when I was first learned to drive as a teenager. It isn't the case when external factors require maximum attention. But because now the act of driving is so second nature, it frees my mind to pursue deeper thought, which often results in a level of creativity that is hard to reproduce at my desk.

An even better example of this is when I am on a treadmill or running on a familiar outdoor path. I don't have to think about what I'm doing. I have been running long enough that my muscle memory takes over and I don't have to actively think about running. The same is true when I'm cycling. I've been a cyclist for many years and there are automatic adjustments to terrain and conditions that I simply no longer have to think about at length.

Both gym time and cycling time are great for creative ideas.

One day I was running around our local park and a great idea came to mind. I stopped, grabbed a twig, and scribbled the idea in the dirt—just in case I could not remember it when I got to my work desk. I at least knew where to go back and find it: in the dirt by the jogging path!

Whether it be typing, running, cycling, or any other task, creating, nurturing and living with mini-patterns can free your mind for creative flashes. Rejoice when they happen!

To Change Your Day . . .

Remember:

- Up to 95 percent of your choices are automatic. Embrace the concept of mini-patterns and begin to isolate key triggers and patterns in your life.

- Incorporate patterns into as many areas of your life and daily schedule as possible.

- Thrivers capitalize on this by intentionally building automatic positive choices into their lives by developing positive mini-patterns into their daily way of life.

- Think about mini-patterns now so you don't have to think about it later.

CHAPTER 12

Emerge from the Fog of Fatigue

Two women were once pitted against each other in a major athletic competition in Hawaii. They each had sacrificed a great deal to be in the competition, and they had virtually no energy left as they faced the final hundred yards of a running course. They had already finished a 2.4-mile ocean swim, cycled 112 miles through the heat and an incessant wind, and were now running the last 1 percent of the way toward the finish line of a marathon run through shadeless lava fields.

In the final 100 yards, each of them had pushed herself beyond her limit. They could no longer run or even walk more than a few paces before they fell to the ground. One of the women, Sian Welch, would stagger and fall to the ground, but as soon as her body touched the ground her mind forced her body to get up, almost as if she bounced off the ground back to a standing position.

Wendy Ingraham, who had caught Sian, also would stagger and fall, but immediately will her body to stand again and walk. The drama of this moment culminated when both Sian and Wendy had fallen only a few meters from the finish line. Both were struggling to stand but were unable. In a flash of creative thinking, Ingraham quit trying to stand and just crawled to the finish line.

She would later say, "All I wanted to do in 1997 was finish that race. Crawling seemed at the time the most efficient way to get to the finish line after endless attempts to walk, run, or even stand up." You could think, *Sure, they are professional athletes, it was the Ironman Triathlon, the biggest race of the year. They were driven to win.* But these two women were competing for fourth place.

I have rarely been more inspired. I came away with the firm conviction that we human beings have far more mental power than most of us realize. We truly can will our bodies

135

to perform feats and endure to a much greater degree than we imagine. For them to push themselves so hard for fourth place reaffirmed my belief that given the right circumstances people we will work hard for a sense of pride and responsibility, and not always for acknowledgment or reward. No one, however, is immune to the physical limit. When your body says that it has had enough, you're done. You may, if you have an iron will, be able to stagger on for a bit, than crawl for a bit more, but it is only a matter of time. Even so, energy is nearly always a renewable resource. Even after a total collapse, the body and mind have a way of replenishing so that a day or so later, a person is again able to "get up and go again." At the end of the race, both women were utterly exhausted, done, bonked, there was nothing left. Yet, after a day's rest from the Ironman, Wendy completed another grueling race the next day with a smile on her face.

HOW MUCH STRUGGLE IS NECESSARY?

Like all who viewed these dramatic moments, you would get so lost in the human drama between these two women that you would likely not notice the other contestants running past this intense struggle, high-fiving the crowd, smiling, cheering, proudly celebrating their success by holding their country's flag high. Other competitors covered the same distance in the same environment, in the same time finished with less struggle and more enjoyment.

How were they able to do this? Given the reputation of both Wendy and Sian, I doubt these people trained harder or were better prepared. Likely what enabled them to accomplish more with less struggle was how they had arranged that particular day. They had likely simply executed their plan better: how much and when they ate and drank, how they paced themselves, and so forth. They probably did not experience the intense competition from their competitors the way Sian and Wendy did. They likely had a great plan, a productive attitude, and followed their plan better, and executed their day a bit differently. The result is that they passed athletes who were likely better trained and had more experience with less stress and effort.

The challenge is to find an ongoing way to replenish and renew energy for a sustained pursuit of goals on a daily basis.

Most professionals, in athletics and business, rarely run out of opportunities to grow, be innovative, focused, healthy, happy, or generous to the people they love. Rather, they often simply run out of the energy they need to capitalize on their opportunities. They have allowed their daily plan and patterns to inadequately recharge their mind, body, and hearts. Some are blindsided by an interruption. But many people simply make an excuse for "not doing" what they value or what they have come to see as motivating. In other words, they begin to take their energy and momentum for granted.

WHY ENERGY IS IMPORTANT TO WORK SUCCESS

Why be concerned with issues related to energy at work?

Because energy is what allows you to get your work done in a timely, high-quality way. And beyond that, having a little excess energy has been shown to:

- Motivate a person to *want* to do their best.
- Make a person more productive and more efficient.
- Increase a person's creativity.
- Lead a person to manifest greater confidence and inspire others to perceive the confident person as a leader.
- Enable a person to regulate their emotions better, as well as their behaviors.
- Make a person more resilient to stress.

- Have more energy after work hours—to connect and contribute more love and attention on family members and friends.

The opposite of energy is fatigue. And living in the fog of fatigue is terrible. Fatigue can keep us from seeing miracles right in front of us. Fatigue can cause a person to act out, lash out, opt out, and miss out!

Fatigue doesn't just cause the body to slow down to a lethargic crawl. It can cause the mind to forget more, make poorer decisions, and be far less creative.

Fatigue directly impacts attitude. It can cause a person to feel overwhelmed, anxious, hopeless, depressed, overly frustrated at minor interruptions, and overburdened by normal responsibilities.

THE THREE VITAL ELEMENTS FOR ENERGY

Energy production is not mysterious. It isn't based on a rocket-science-style formula. Energy requires three things:

1. Food
2. Sleep
3. Activity—physical, and also mental

Each of these elements must be present in both quantity and quality, ideally at *optimal* levels.

Countless research studies have affirmed that food, sleep, and physical exertion (enhanced by mental exertion) directly impact energy levels.

A Florida State University study found that when blood sugar levels drop and a person becomes "too hungry," self-control drops significantly. (Self-control is another way of saying willpower.)

A researcher at Stanford found that people are more susceptible to cravings if they sleep less than six hours a night. In other words, sleep deprivation and food binges are linked. A lack of sleep impacts energy, and the food is a perceived way to compensate for energy input.

My Core Concept for this has three prongs: eat smart, sleep deep, and exert positive motion.

Core Concepts: Eat Smart, Sleep Deep, and Exert Positive Motion

On the next several pages, I want to explore with you the tremendous advantages that come from these three Core Concepts.

1. **Smart Eating**. Food is the body's source of fuel. Food has a direct and immediate effect on a person's mood, ability to concentrate, and the ability to address and solve problems.

2. **Deep Sleep**. Sleep is the ultimate body, mind, and mood regenerator. Sleep helps "reboot" the mind to restore memory, perception, and general thinking abilities. During sleep, the body repairs cellular damage after an active day.

3. **Positive Exertion (Movement)**. Physical activity improves a person's overall coordination—including "mental coordination." It strengthens a person's physical being at all levels, from the cell to physical organs to total-body physiological systems. Physical exertion releases and removes important chemicals (such as adrenalin, cortisol, and melatonin) so that a person can function in an optimal way, both physically and mentally. Exercise also releases endorphins that make exertion pleasurable, and releases neurotransmitter hormones that increase the production of T cells that are the basis for a strong immune system.

(continued)

(continued)
Insights into Smart Eating

When and what you eat impacts your mental function far more than most people realize. A study was done involving courtroom judges, and more specifically, judges who were responsible for granting or denying parole. Researchers found that if a person came before a parole board at a time of day when blood sugar levels tended to be optimal, a person had a 65 percent chance of being paroled.

However, if a person came before a parole board that was hungry, with suboptimal blood-sugar levels, the person's chances of parole dropped dramatically, eventually hitting less than a 10 percent chance! After the parole board members took a break to eat and replenish their blood sugar levels, the chances of parole bounced back up to 60 to 65 percent.

It appears that even dedicated, educated, and responsible people can be greatly influenced by blood-sugar chemistry, even if they are totally unaware of the phenomenon at work in their bodies.

Blood-sugar levels can impact a person's ability to think clearly or make good choices. Again, most people are likely to blame a number of other factors before they ever get around to eating patterns.

So what's the conclusion?

To be a Thriver, a person needs to establish an overall daily pattern of eating that allows for multiple, planned "refueling breaks." Each intake of food needs to include quality protein and a portion of complex carbohydrates (vegetables, fruits, whole grains), and limited additional sugars. That's the basic eating pattern for high energy and an even blood sugar that enhances creativity, decision-making ability, and motivation.

What about Caffeine? I know a number of people who advise NO caffeine in the workplace. I am not one of those. I have learned through the years that Thrivers often use caffeine to significantly improve performance.

Are you aware that even moderately high caffeine intake can get an Olympic athlete stripped of medals or thrown out of the

Olympic Games? It's true. Only 300 to 400 mg of caffeine (three to four eight-ounce cups of strong coffee) has been shown to:

- Increase strength by 7 percent.
- Increase endurance by 20 percent.
- Significantly reduce chances of making mistakes when fatigued.
- Speed up reaction time.
- Improve short-term memory.

Too much caffeine on any one day can cause problems, but studies are showing that around four cups of coffee a day can have positive health results that include a preventive effect against heart disease, diabetes, several types of cancer, Alzheimer's disease, and even dental cavities! An amount of 300 to 400 mg has shown little evidence of health risk, and some bona fide health and mental benefits.

I'm not talking about caramel frap-o-latte beverages. Sugar intake with caffeine is another ballgame.

The benefits of caffeine are also not for everyone. Some people are more sensitive to caffeine, and of course caffeine is not advised for pregnant women, heart patients, people with high blood pressure, children, the elderly, or those at risk for osteoporosis.

A person who exhibits the following symptoms should ease back on caffeine or cut it out completely: insomnia, tremors, nausea, vomiting, chest pains, and heart palpitations.

Insights into Getting a Good Night's Sleep

It really is no accident that we say "good night" to one another, or that we often ask a person early in morning, "Did you get a good night's sleep?"

Every person desires a period of sleep that is sufficiently long and of high quality. Length and quality are what make a sleep session "good"!

(continued)

(*continued*)

Lost sleep is considered by sleep researchers to be incurred as a *debt*. Even staying up 20 minutes later at night can build a sleep indebtedness that can turn into long-haul exhaustion. Sleep debt can reduce levels of leptin (a substance secreted by fat cells that reduces appetite) and cause increased cravings for junk foods. Sleep debt can cause a bad attitude, a sharp decline of natural antibodies (as much as a 50 percent drop) that leaves a person more susceptible to colds and flu, higher blood pressure, and insulin resistance, and even an increase in heart disease, stroke, and diabetes.

Some people claim that they can get by on five hours of sleep a night. That's only an illusion. There is no scientific research to back up that such a low amount of sleep is healthful.

A study of Stanford University basketball players showed that those athletes who accepted the challenge to get 90 minutes more sleep a night found that they had a 9 percent increase in their ability to make both free throws and three-point shots. They also reported feeling less fatigued during the day, and reported a higher sense of well-being and improved overall mood.

If you mentioned to a college basketball coach that you could improve his athletes' shooting percentage by 9 percent without increasing practice time, he or she would think you are a crackpot.

How can you tell if you are sleep deprived?

Common sense answers are if it is hard to wake up, if you are getting excessively sleepy in the afternoon, and one of my favorites is how long it takes you to fall asleep, which is called sleep latency. Most sleep experts agree that "normal" is somewhere between 15 and 20 minutes. If you fall asleep faster than 5 or maybe even 10 minutes, getting more, quality sleep needs to become a priority.

Mini-Patterns Can Help! "Going to bed earlier for longer, deeper sleep" is a good goal. It's a worthy change. But this isn't just a matter of piling into your bed at a specific hour. There are a number of subtasks that can and should become part of a mini-pattern that might loosely be labeled "the going-to-bed mini-pattern."

Such a pattern might include taking a warm bath, perhaps in aromatic bath salts that invite relaxation . . . turning on soothing music and turning off the television . . . setting out food items and clothing for the next morning, as well as items that must be in the briefcase or next to the exit door—all of which can make a morning go more smoothly and keep a person from thinking about these things during the night . . . and perhaps making a list of the next day's two or three main goals.

Such a pattern of small tasks can add up to create a winding-down mini-pattern that is very effective and relaxing. And for many people, giving thanks for the good things of the day, and forgiving those who may need forgiving for the hurt they've caused. These are all tasks that can provide great benefit when they become part of a preparing-for-sleep pattern. Furthermore, these are bite-sized pieces, each of which takes only a few minutes (except for that *long* soaking bath, of course!).

To get great sleep, a person must manage these three variables:

1. Darkness. The brain translates darkness as "time to sleep." Turn off all the lights you can turn off, especially overhead lights. Instead use lamps, candles, or other soft, unobtrusive sources of light.

2. Coolness. Turn down the thermostat several degrees.

3. A predictable bedtime routine that sends strong signals to the brain that it is time to shut off the day and relax into sleep. As part of that routine—a mini-pattern—you might consider softer lighting for two hours before bedtime.

Also, fast for 12 to 14 hours before your desired wake-up time. In other words, if you want to wake up at seven in the morning, try to eat very little if at all after seven the night before. Make sure there's protein in your last meal of the day to help you outlast blood-sugar lows in the middle of the night.

(continued)

(*continued*)

I also strongly suggest that before going to sleep, kiss anything that could use a kiss, even your pets. Say "I love you." Voice words of appreciation and gratitude to those you live with. You'll sleep better and so will they.

The Snooze Button is Secretly Plotting to Destroy You

When you were a kid and were playing at a park and your mom or dad yelled, "Honey, time to go," how did you respond? Probably, "Awww! Just 5 more minutes, okay?" My kids do it, I did it, and I bet you did too. You just want a little more time. You think that little more time is going make a difference. That after 5 more minutes you'll be ready to go. But alas, that is not so. When the 5 minutes are up, you ask with even a little more urgency for "just" 5 more. And then just 5 more . . . And, when the time was finally up and you had to leave, were you ready? Maybe, but I doubt it. I bet you were just as ticked off if not more so than if your mom had you leave the first time she mentioned it.

How many times do you routinely hit the snooze bar or button on your alarm clock on the average morning? Just five more minutes sounds like such a good idea. In truth, however, a pattern of snoozing "just a few more minutes" has been shown to make a person *more* tired, not less. A few minutes of early-morning stretching is far more advantageous in helping a person rise rested and ready to go than five minutes more shallow sleep.

The Best Exercise on the Planet

I've asked thousands of health professionals, "What is the best exercise on the planet?" Almost without exception, they will respond with "walking!" Walking is a wonderful exercise, and arguably the most convenient. Is it the best?

Which activity produces athletes with the most fit heart and lungs? Cross-country skiing. So, is that the best exercise?

Which activity burns the most calories per minute? Running. Is running the best?

Which physical activity is the most enjoyable? Sex, for sure. Normal intercourse (yeah, I know, define normal) has been measured to require about 7 METS, which is to say the same effort as light jogging. Is it the best? The problem here is duration.

Many choices to be sure, but again, what is the best exercise on the planet? The answer is—the one you will do. I'm not being a smart alec, well, a little, but my point is it does not matter how good an exercise is for you if you don't do it.

Answer: It is the exercise most people will do, and do consistently!

A regular exercise routine has been shown to reduce the chance of getting some forms of cancer by up to 22 percent. It has been shown to reduce the risk of type 2 diabetes. It has also been shown to enhance memory.

In one study a group of participants read two paragraphs, waited 35 minutes, and then were asked questions about what they had read. Another group exercised for 40 minutes, read two paragraphs, waited 35 minutes, and were asked questions. The exercise group was able to remember significantly more than the nonexercise group!

A Penn State study confirmed those results for college students taking exams.

So how much exercise does a person need to get good mental benefits? Between 20 and 60 minutes of moderate exertion.

The next time you feel your memory stumbling—go for a long brisk walk!

Studies have shown that even 15 minutes of walking can strengthen resolve to avoid temptations, boost a positive attitude, and reduce stress. The benefits of exercise actually start at the five-minute mark!

I find it greatly encouraging that more and more people are engaged in MBWA—management by walking around. They might personally walk through their entire department or division, stopping for small mini-meetings with various workers along the way.

(continued)

(continued)

Others do their "walking around" with colleagues or employees and use this as meeting time on specific issues or topics.

There is a large and growing body of empirical evidence that show that people who exercise experience significant, if not astonishingly large, increases in productivity.

H.A.L.T. When You Need To

There's a well-known "rule" in psychology that says, "Don't allow yourself to become too hungry, too angry, too lonely (isolated or disconnected from others), or too tired." The initial letters of this advice spell out H-A-L-T. You must take action to avoid becoming sluggish, or even discouraged or depressed. You must eat regularly, and find ways to release your anger that don't involve pain to yourself, pain to others, or destruction of property. You must keep communication going with others who will affirm you and encourage you. You must get sufficient sleep. To do less is to invite problems!

The good news is that most people in the United States have the ability to control how they think and live. You can choose when to wake, eat, and sleep. Most people *can* learn to manage their anger, and replace hateful and bitter responses to life with responses that are psychologically healthy. If you have an anger problem, get help for it. You may very well lengthen your life, and even if not, you can certainly improve the quality of your own life and the lives of others around you if you will learn to channel your anger into productive activities.

H.A.L.T. is not something that others can *make* you do. It is something you must do for yourself as a part of adopting a positive daily schedule.

So, as the commercial says, "Just do it."

To Change Your Day . . .

Remember:

- You probably run out of energy before you run out of opportunities. Thrivers are better at managing their energy than Strivers.

- Set in place an overall daily regimen of eating five to six small "meals." For most people, it is three squares (well-balanced meals) and two snacks. The key is to eat something every three hours you are awake.

- Develop a deep sleep mini-pattern. Set in place an overall daily regimen that allows you to get sufficient, quality sleep.

- Set in place an overall daily regimen that includes active physical exercise—brisk walking is great, but start with whatever you will do more often!

An overall healthy daily routine enables you to stay far more motivated in accomplishing mini-patterns that boost both energy and momentum.

CHAPTER 13

Maximizing Your Mini-Patterns

There are several times in every day that seem to cry out for mini-patterns. While the advice in this chapter is not extensive, there's enough here to make a significant impact in just about any person's day.

Maximize Your Morning. There's a very simple little mini-pattern that helps many people get a better start to a day: Food first, caffeine second.

I enjoy my morning coffee, but I know from experience and research that the best thing I can do to get my daily eating plan off on the right note is to eat first—a mix of protein and carbs—and then have caffeine.

Maximize Your Work Breaks. Thomas Edison once said he never solved his problems while he was in his laboratory, but instead, when he went for a walk and snacked on an apple. In many cases you are likely to find that a step away from a problem allows you to see it with new eyes. A break can help you gain insights and give clarity to issues, problems, and decisions. I like what François Gautier has said: "More important than the quest for certainty is the quest for clarity."

Seek to make the most of your "breaks" at work.

A 2011 study conducted at Portland State University and the University of Michigan interviewed 214 workers. Workers were asked to identify the top five things they did to stay energized at work, while still doing their work. They said:

1. Check e-mail.
2. Switch to another task.
3. Make a to-do list.
4. Offer help to someone at work.
5. Talk to a coworker or supervisor.

The sad fact is that none of these activities actually increased energy and vitality. Not one.

On the other hand, the following eight "break-time" activities did increase vitality:

1. Learn something new.
2. Focus for a few moments on what gives you joy in your work.
3. Set a new goal.
4. Do something to make a colleague happy.
5. Express gratitude to someone you work with.
6. Seek feedback.
7. Reflect on how you make a difference by the work you do.
8. Reflect on the meaning of your work.

These activities, even if activated for only a few minutes, were associated with less fatigue and higher reported feelings of vitality.

Maximize Your Lunch Break—In Fact, Take Two Lunch Breaks. Most people have a designated time in their workday for "lunch." How you define lunch can set you up for a lethargic or highly productive afternoon. I strongly encourage people to take a break at noon or the equivalent if you don't work the typical 8-to-5 workday, but to do so in a way that keeps their energy and momentum flowing.

Here are several strategies to consider:

- Actually have lunch! Don't work through lunch, or eat lunch while you are working. Take a lunch break.
- Make conscious choices about what is healthful, and also choose to eat light. Think of lunch as a snack—and plan to have another snack at 3 o'clock. This enables you to think: "Eat light."

I personally like broth-based soups. The crockpot in our kitchen at home nearly always has a soup brewing.

Broth-based soups can usually be found at most restaurants, including the ones at airports. Look for ones with veggies added.

Salads are great for lunch—especially ones loaded with beans, peppers, and other vegetables, and a form of protein, such as egg, chicken, tuna, or turkey. Be careful in choosing a salad dressing. Highly processed and high-fat dressings should be avoided. I usually use balsamic vinegar or vinegar and oil as a dressing.

If you are having a sandwich, make it a big one and cut it in half so you can save that second half for your 3-o'clock "second lunch."

- Share lunch with someone you enjoy talking with and listening to. Choose people who make you laugh and who are interesting to you.
- Rather than share lunch with a person you *don't* enjoy, choose solitude and make your lunch break a time for quiet reflection. That's far more energizing than spending time with someone you find irritating, negative, or yawn-producing boring.
- Encourage workplace potlucks. They add variety and fun and there is growing scientific evidence that suggests they increase productivity and employee engagement.
- When you are using your lunch break to socialize with colleagues, avoid talking about projects or the workplace. I have only one rule for company lunches: "no talky about worky." It's not a break if you talk shop—it's a meeting.
- Mix up your lunch plans. Perhaps use three lunches a week for exercising, and two for socializing. Go different places. Go with different people.
- Give yourself "credit" for a lunch break well spent. Don't see lunch time as a "waste" or as a filler. Don't even see it as an intermission between morning productivity and afternoon productivity. Rather, see it as a valuable task period in its own right. Reward yourself for spending the time wisely.

- When the clock strikes 3, stop for your "second lunch." For many people, the most important meal of the day is a 3-o'clock snack! Try to have about 40 grams of complex carbohydrates and some protein. This will significantly boost your energy level and concentration, curb your sugar cravings, and give you better appetite control for dinner.

    What makes for a good mid-afternoon snack? Consider a half cup of Greek yogurt and two slices of no-sugar-added pineapple; a half cup of nonfat cottage cheese and a half of a bell pepper; a small packet of tuna and half a tomato; or my favorite, the Peanut Butter Halfie, which is simply a piece of whole grain bread smeared with a dollop of peanut butter and then folded over.

Maximize Your Life "On the Road." Maintaining changes and new mini-patterns on the road can be tough. Let me give you three suggestions:

1. *Socialization.* Sharing your meals and exercise time with friends and coworkers along the way is one of the most rewarding things you can do. It adds fun to your travel and also keeps you more accountable. You are much less likely to skip a workout if you have set an appointment to exercise with someone at your travel destination. The key is to pre-plan your exercise times.
2. *Systematize Your Schedule.* A trade show or meeting schedule has set times for various events. You can adopt this same idea for your personal time and overall scheduling. Put your life on autopilot according to a plan. Take your exercise or eating logs or other journals with you and keep them up to date. It will help you stay on track.
3. *Lighten Up.* Don't beat yourself up if you miss something along the way. Putting too much pressure on yourself to get all things accomplished "on the road" may do more

harm than good. Be open and prepared to seize opportunities for exercise or shared meals. Put emphasis on getting enough sleep.

In my opinion, travel is hardest on a sleep schedule, especially if you are crossing several time zones. There are a few things you can do to help yourself.

Australian researchers found that light applied to the back of a person's knees can help reset a sleep/wake cycle. This does not seem very practical to me, however, and it is just plain weird. But it worked.

In my opinion, this is a better approach:

- Determine what time you need to wake up. Then 12 hours before your wake time, start fasting.
- As soon as you awaken, exercise.
- Eat a healthy, hearty breakfast with a good mix of protein and carbohydrates.
- Repeat tomorrow.

It is true at all times but it seems especially important to remember as you travel that perception drives your physical reactions. I encourage you to think like a world-class skier. Such a skier can look from the top of a mountain down an icy, dangerous slope, and think, "Wow—what a run this will be!" They see challenge and excitement, and feel only a motivating twinge of fear.

See your travel as an adventure, not a chore. Change your attitude from one of "got to" to "get to." Choose to see interruptions and delays as part of the adventure, and an opportunity to meet new people, learn new things, and perhaps even catch up on paperwork or calls.

Maximize Your "End of Day" Mini-Pattern. The vast majority of people I've coached through the years have heard me say, "You can't get to the top of the slide without climbing the stairs." Fantastic days are *built*, they don't just automatically appear. There is always effort in "getting going" on a new day.

Preparation for that begins the night before!

Core Concept: Prepare for tomorrow morning *before* you go home or go to bed.

Let me give you several practical suggestions related to this:

- Before you leave work for the day, make sure you have laid out the first project you want to address the following morning. That might mean retrieving a particular file folder, making some notes on a blank piece of paper, or making a short list of specific steps you anticipate taking as you pursue the next morning's "hot project" (such as phone calls to make, information to request, or facts to revisit). Having the start of your workday ready acts as a positive trigger that initiates as soon as you arrive. Think about it today so you don't have to think about it tomorrow.

- Leave your work at work. Stay until you reach a good stopping place, and then stop.

- Get rid of as much of the day's stress as you can before you arrive at home. One of my clients changes into more relaxed clothes *before* he begins his commute home—this might enable you to walk around the block after you pull into your driveway and before you open the door to your house.

- Do something that amounts to play! My little girls love to dance, and there are a couple of television programs for children that are geared to dance. It is not unusual for me to arrive home to hear pleas from my daughters, "Come dance with me!" Dancing definitely helps me define the end of a workday and the start of an evening at home with my family. Find an energizing transition from work to your personal time.

- Only take work home that you know you can do in a prescribed amount of time, and with good concentration. I have met a number of people who take home "reports" or "professional articles" to read and digest in the evening hours. They often admit to falling asleep in a big easy chair after reading only the first few pages. If something takes focused concentration or involves important decision making, the evening hours at home may not be the prime time. On the other hand, if you are a night owl and can sleep in the next morning, and if you seem to reenergize under the glow of a bright lightbulb and do your best creating after the house is quiet, at-home late-night work might be for you! Just be sure you don't amass a sleep debt.

MIX IT UP!

To have mini-patterns in place does not necessarily equate to being in a rut. Mixing up the order in a mini-pattern can be good, or doing things in a slightly different way or in a different environment can keep the routine itself from becoming boring.

Variety is motivating.

Scout out a new walking or jogging or cycling trail.

Try new recipes and new spices or herbs.

Change that is enjoyable sends a reinforcing signal to the brain: the more difficult changes you are seeking to make can be enjoyable too!

USE JOURNALING TO YOUR ADVANTAGE

I am a huge advocate for the benefits that come from journaling. You are probably already doing it in one form or another. You might think of this as keeping a log, record keeping, writing a planning document, and so forth. A journal can be used to document virtually every aspect of life. It can take the form of a budget or financial recordkeeping. It can keep track of exercise or weight. It can be a place for writing down new ideas. It can be a statement of goals and plans related to them.

THE COUNTERINTUITIVE STARTING POINT

One of the greatest benefits to journaling is it helps clarify your thinking. It is often prescribed by psychologists to their patients as a way to help ferret out the root causes of many stressful situations. Journaling is an exceptional introspective tool to help a person see more clearly when and how problems developed that brought about a damaging, undesirable, or injurious situation or relationship. Here is the counterintuitive suggestion—journal about when things were good. When you can identify when things were *right*, you have a much clearer understanding of when things went wrong!

That's true for both personal and work situations. It can be the most important starting point possible for real systems changes on the job or at home. It can be the key to identifying marital or parenting difficulties, employee conflicts, and employee-administrative differences, as well as improving company-customer, company-vendor, and other workplace relationships that go beyond the walls of the home office.

Describing when things were good can function a little like a "System Restore Point" on a computer, which is when your computer takes a snapshot of itself. This is most often done when a computer is working optimally, so that if a problem arises, the user can simply instruct the computer to "restore" itself to the previous point and within a few minutes the computer is back to its previous, optimal state. I frequently coach people to establish a "Lifestyle Restore Point."

Lifestyle Restore Point. A Lifestyle Restore Point is a snapshot of the way your life is *when it is working well*. What does your day look like? How are you feeling? What are you doing? What changes did you make? By documenting what's working well and doesn't need changing, you create a tool you can use in the future.

If you "fall off the wagon," you can consult your journal to see how you were living and thinking previously and have a clear guide to "restore" yourself to previous successes and conclude, "I've done this before, I can do it again!"

To Change Your Day . . .

Make the most of mini-patterns throughout an entire day.

CHAPTER **14**

Tips for Times When Demands Are Exceptionally Great

Does your company ever throw a BHAG at you? Many companies do.

BHAG is an acronym for "Big Hairy Audacious Goal." It might be a new software system. It might be a sales goal. It might be a productivity goal, or perhaps a new efficiency or quality standard. The point is that the goal is so big that it is on the brink of unrealistic, and few know at the outset that it can actually be reached.

When a BHAG is announced, it rarely brings applause or big smiles. Rather, it usually produces a worrisome silence. And in the wake of its announcement, a BHAG produces stress—lots of stress, in lots of areas, for most of the people involved.

What can one person do in the midst of this? How is a BHAG to be conquered?

First, in the face of a BHAG goal, you must make up your mind that you are going to believe the goal can be reached—somehow. A BHAG is a challenge, not a threat.

Second, define the key goals that will help you accomplish the BHAG. You climb Mt. Everest by reaching the first base camp, then the next-highest camp, and so forth.

Third, and the most overlooked step, is to break down those goals in a way that you can accomplish them via your daily routine or a daily checklist. A task takes on a sense of drudgery—a huge drain on energy and momentum—if you believe you are pursuing a lost cause or are working under pressure to succeed at a level that even your top boss doesn't think can be reached.

STAY IN TOUCH WITH YOUR CORE

I like what Raymond Hull once said: "He who trims himself to suit everyone else will soon whittle himself away."

CeeLo Green, a noted musician, once said, "I've tried to be so many people for so many people. When you truly accept yourself for who you are, it is an unconditional kind of love."

There comes a point when each person needs to say, "I cannot do more than I can do in order to please other people." It is important to know yourself, your limits, and how to be true to you.

The truth is, most people can do more than they think they can do. Most people can change and grow. Most people can learn new skills, adapt to new schedules, and manage their work in new ways. Even if they are already at a very high level.

But it is equally true that there comes a point when a person cannot change their core values and still be who they are! You cannot change your most basic spiritual, emotional, or intellectual nature. To do so is to lose your uniqueness and, eventually, your "edge."

You need to have a touchstone in high-demand times to remind you of who you are and where you are in a given period of your life. You need to identify—and revisit when necessary—a personal "reference point" to determine if you are on the right track in your job, career, or personal life.

My family calls me "directionally impaired." That's a nice way of saying that I don't have a great sense of direction when driving. The problem seems greater when I'm driving in town than when I'm in another town or out on open roads. The fortunate thing for me is that my home town is Fayetteville, Arkansas, and the University of Arkansas is on top of a large hill. The tower of the building called "Old Main" can be seen from much of the city. So, when I'm driving and I need to regain my sense of direction, I often can simply look up and find Old Main. I regain my bearings and have renewed confidence—and ability—that I can find my way.

What gives you your bearings when you begin to wonder, "Why am I working so hard?" or "Why am I sacrificing so much?" or "Why am I not happier?" in your current job.

Just saying, "I've got to pay my bills" is not a sufficient reason. Financial responsibility is important, but it is rarely what gives you energizing and motivating reasons to work hard over a long period of time.

Your own sense of personal values is likely to be Old Main for you. Make sure your own values are in focus. Be able to list them and quickly reference them. They can give you meaning on days that seem void of meaning.

REMOVE OR ELIMINATE SOMETHING

One day while I was playing with my daughter Bella, who was about 10 months old at the time, I noticed a pattern developing. Bella had a few toys in front of her. She would pick up one small toy with one hand and bring it close to her eyes and give it her total attention. Then she would spot a second toy. She would reach for it and hold it close with her other hand. A few moments later, a third toy captured her eye. But now she had a problem—both of her hands were full. What could she do?

She instantly and instinctively dropped one of the first two toys and reached for the third. She continued to do this, again and again, going from one of the three toys to another. And the more she did this, the more dissatisfied and fussy she became. What was the answer?

Some people might suggest giving her more or different toys. Some might suggest you limit the amount of time she can spend with any one toy. But the approach that is advocated by many child psychologists is to *take away* toys!

I implemented this tactic and she rebelled, as I had expected. But then, to my amazement, she became quieter and happier and more satisfied. When she had only two toys to consider, they were sufficient. First one was held close to her eyes so that she could examine it, and then the other. She appeared to thoroughly enjoy evaluating each of them, repeatedly. She was no longer overwhelmed by options.

A common characteristic of Thrivers is that they are able to stay focused on a task until it is finished. Many people in the workplace seem to me to be overwhelmed by their options on any given day. They have a long to-do list expected of them or, in the case of the self-employed, they themselves think they should accomplish a great number of things.

Very often a person in this situation will pick up one task, work at it for a short while, and then pick up another task that seems equally urgent. And so on and on it goes: the worker becomes more and more dissatisfied at getting nothing truly *accomplished*—and tends to become crankier and more frustrated as the workday draws to a close. All "fun" has gone of work at that point and, in most cases, the person finds it difficult to gain any kind of momentum or traction the following morning with many partially done projects that are scattered on the desktop.

Artists have noted that if they leave a canvas prematurely—according to whatever degree of work they had hoped to accomplish in a given time period—it may take several hours or days to get back into an equally productive state, if it happens at all. The same can and does happen in negotiations—both political and financial. Unplanned interruptions and delays have a negative impact, often slowing down the entire process, and it takes considerable energy and focus to get things back on track and moving forward.

An interruption during an exercise session almost always prematurely ends a workout.

THE VALUE OF SOCIALIZATION

I recently was working with a company that had gone through a very difficult financial time from 2009 to 2011. Their organization had provided good guidance, but many of the employees—mostly women—had each been encouraged to run a leaner operation. In essence, each woman ran her own "franchise" in this company, so she had control over her own overhead. In previous years, the mother company had recommended that a franchisee have one in-person office assistant. When tough financial times occurred, the company switched its recommendation and encouraged the elimination of the in-person office assistant and encouraged virtual assistants. In essence, each woman was expected to be an island unto herself.

Happiness and job satisfaction plummeted.

Gallup-Healthways polled more than 140,000 people and found that a person's ability to function at his or her best was directly correlated to how much they socialized during a day.

We are social creatures and we need interaction.

Working *with* other people—and communicating with others in the normal course of the day—results in less stress and worry, and more happiness and enjoyment.

The franchisee who heard the results associated with "low socialization" immediately agreed with the findings. The women admitted openly that they were not having as much face-to-face time as they needed, and that the loss of an office assistant had not impacted their task accomplishments nearly as much as it had impacted their levels of personal stress, worry, and happiness.

The sad fact is that the more we feel stressed, the more we withdraw from others.

I asked an attendee at a recent meeting what he did to socialize. He confidently replied that he played golf with friends. I asked him to tell me about the last time he played.

He thought for a moment, and then replied, "Well, I *used* to play golf."

When we find ourselves under tight demands and great pressure, we must not withdraw. Rather, the smart thing to do is to reach out to others—extend our connection time with family members and friends. The socialization can be energizing, and give a glow of reward to the hard hours of sheer slogging.

A lack of feelings of social support can negatively impact a person's motivation. On the other hand, feeling social support—and especially from people you like or love, and people who are good role models—can greatly impact your own motivation, which can be especially true in times of high work demand.

Assess Your "Team." Who is on your team, at work and in your personal life? How do you interact with these people? What do they give to you in terms of encouragement and help?

You very likely do not need critics in your life. You know when you are doing badly or are failing. If you need information, or help in acquiring a skill, seek it. As much as possible, distance yourself from the naysayers and the critics. To maintain your own positive energy, you need to be in association with positive people.

You may not be able to decide who is going to be on your team at work, or at home. But you can decide how much interaction you are going to allow yourself to have with negative people, and you can register a goal with others that you want your interactions to be positive, encouraging, and focused on the good that exists and that lies ahead. Sometimes simply saying to others on your team, "Let's change our collective attitude" can be a huge step in the right direction.

Monitor your own role-modeling. Seek to become the positive, encouraging person you hope others will be to you. Display the behaviors of kindness and mercy. Give words that are genuinely helpful or complimentary. Role-modeling does not only positively influence others, but also serves as a trigger internally to continue the behavior.

Social Media. When I ask people in workshops if they think that social media helps a person stay firmly connected to others, less than 10 percent believe so. I certainly use Facebook, LinkedIn, and Twitter. But I do so to convey information that is mutually beneficial, as well as simply to "talk" with the people in my circles. I believe that social media *can* enhance socialization and social connections, but it is rarely a one-to-one comparison of time to value received as can occur with in-person interactions. If you often feel like you are going it alone or that you are more stressed or less happy than you think you should be, and are not spending much quality time with others (not only those you love and like, but also peers who have similar work and life demands as you), I suggest that you build more face-to-face, heart-to-heart time into your day.

Besides the major social media sites, there are a number of specialized social sites that place high emphasis on encouragement and motivation. I recommend you seek out one as a possible source of help to you as you pursue a new goal or seek to make a specific change in your daily patterns. For example, SparkPeople is an online weight-loss community. Researchers who analyzed their data concluded that 88 percent were using the site for encouragement and motivation, while 59 percent used it as a source of information, and 43 percent as an outlet for sharing experiences. The high emphasis on positive encouragement resulted in real benefit for the vast majority of those accessing the site regularly.

Goal Partners. Most people can benefit greatly from working toward a goal with another person, and especially with two other people. "Going it alone" is tough.

Rather than think in terms of accountability partners, I like to think in terms of "Goal Partners." Find someone who wants to reach his or her goal as much as you want to reach yours, and ideally in the same area of goal pursuit! Share how you are changing your day to move yourself one small step at a time toward that goal. Encourage one another in the process. Be an in-person and virtual part of each other's day.

ADOPT A MINI-PATTERN OF APPRECIATION CONVERSATIONS

"Why am I so much more stressed or less happy than I should be based on how my life is going?"

I hear this question a lot, especially among Strivers and Strugglers. The questions I ask in return are, "Are you truly thankful for your life? Are you thankful for the people in your life, the work you get to do, the things you are able to enjoy? How often do you think about and talk about what you are grateful for?"

In my experience, Thrivers are significantly more grateful for what they experience in life. This is backed up by a multitude of research studies that have shown significant benefits to cultivating an attitude of appreciation, including:

- Better health
- Less anxiety and depression
- Sounder sleep
- Higher long-term satisfaction with life

Feed and re-feed your mind with gratitude. Appreciation is a great way to bookend many different activities in life. Finish work, exercise, dinner . . . with appreciation. My father-in-law is a pastor and he begins each meal with a prayer of appreciation. What about a personal practice of making appreciation your closing thought?

These moments of appreciation are also often moments of reflections on "meaning"—a known re-energizer for mind and body.

I recommend starting "Appreciation Conversations." At the end of the day, I often ask my office manager for her "Best plays of the day," and I show sincere appreciation for her. When I put my kids to bed, the last thing we talk about is what we are grateful for, and I show sincere appreciation for them. In the quiet hours of the evening, my wife and I will often begin conversations of what we are grateful about, including our family, work, home, etc., and I show sincere appreciation for her. Right before you sleep, making appreciation your last thought is also strongly related to happiness. My trigger is when I start to feel sleepy. I then put my book down on the bedside table and think about what I'm thankful for that day. Then, I'm out like a light. This is a great way to end the day.

ADOPT STRATEGIES FOR ENERGIZING YOURSELF AND OTHERS AROUND YOU

Especially in BHAG times, every person on a team needs to agree that they will do their utmost to energize one another as much as possible. There are five simple strategies that can help with this:

1. Set a new personal goal and begin to chase it—even a small goal. This is more energizing than reorganizing your to-do list or feeling totally preoccupied with the BHAG.
2. Engage your mind with *learning*, not worrying or winning.
3. Everybody needs to vent their anxiety or anger at times, but don't do it at work. Energy comes from seeking and giving quality feedback, and channeling all feelings of anxiety and anger into genuine listening and learning.
4. Reflect on what gives you joy and meaning. A few moments of this can energize you more than a break-room snack. Share what gives you joy and meaning with a coworker who is receptive to hearing what you have to share.

5. Help more than you offer. Giving real help to others and showing concern for them is energizing both to the person doing the giving and the one who receives. Offering help to someone does not always have the same effect. Sometimes people are too busy to think about how you can help them. I'm not saying that you shouldn't offer help, but make sure are not giving someone another "to do."

DEVELOP A MOTIVE TO "SERVE"

Imagine that you are backstage in a large auditorium. You are standing in semidarkness, although you can hear clearly what is going on outside in the "house." More than 900 people are present—they are the top 1 percent of a very successful company—and you are about to speak to them. At that moment, the event planner comes up with a nervous expression and tense body language and says, "The CEO is sitting left center on the front row. No pressure." She walks away. You know she is not trying to make you nervous—rather, *she* is nervous. But you also know that she has a lot riding on this event and on your presentation.

Just as she walks away, another person walks up briskly and whispers, "The first speaker went way long. Can you cut your speech down from 60 minutes to 45 minutes?" You agree— what else *can* you do? You quickly begin going through what you had *planned* to say in an attempt to make changes.

And then the organizer checks her watch and says, "You are on in five, four, three . . ."

People who have studied fear routinely report that "public speaking" is one of the top five fears reported by adults in the United States.

By "public" they generally mean more than the number of people who can be seated a conference table.

Much of my work involves public speaking. Am I nervous before I speak? My answer is, "Thankfully, yes." I have learned to channel my "stage fright" into added energy and to a greater vocal and physical dynamic.

Early in my career I was fortunate to hear Dr. Terry Paulson, a hall of fame professional speaker, who advised, "If you are ever feeling overly nervous, you need to recite a simple prayer, 'Please, Lord, let me serve and not shine.'"

Serve and Not Shine. Those four words completely transformed my approach to public speaking. They allowed me to get me out of the way. They allowed me to shift from being overly concerned with whether people liked me and to focus on what I might do to help my audience members reach their goals and be at their best.

Being one who serves *can* and *will* be the key to ultimately shining.

In sales, for example, one of the biggest rookie mistakes salespeople make is focusing on how they can shine. They seek to make more sales to have more money and more recognition. Perhaps you have encountered a salesperson who projects "How can I sell this to you?" with the hidden subtext of "So I can make my quota this month."

It is a rare salesman who says, "What do you need?" It's not as much a matter of *technique* as it is of *attitude*!

Generally, in the workplace a major atmosphere shift occurs when a person begins to see others around him or her as having areas of weakness or needs that might be *helped*, rather than seeing every other employee as a competitor (even while knowing that you are all working for the same organization) or as a fellow companion on a sinking ship.

If you see yourself in a situation that has no good outcome, the tendency is going to be "every person for himself or herself." That is precisely the *wrong* approach to take. Think instead, *Serve and Not Shine*.

Serving others requires a shift of focus toward the way you work, rather than the outcome of your work. It requires a shift in focus from feeling threatened or "under fire" at work, to feeling challenged and useful.

The person who seeks to serve is nearly always respected, included, and considered valuable!

And those are great "rewards"—*especially* in times when demand is high.

To Change Your Day . . .

Remember:

- Think of BHAGs as challenges, not threats.

- Thrivers value and make true social connections and personal interactions a part of their day.

- Put renewed emphasis on socialization, communication, and service to your peers.

- Refuse to complain. Instead, infuse your day with expressions of appreciation and gratitude.

- Make it a goal to change the atmosphere in your workplace or home to one of relational strength, not stress. Remember to serve, and not shine.

CHAPTER 15

Staying in the Flow of the Process

I feel certain that if you have watched a professional basketball game at least a few times, you will be able to imagine the scene I'm going to describe.

Michael Jordan, past superstar for the Chicago Bulls, was facing certain defeat at the hands of a rival team. His team was down only two points, but there were mere seconds remaining in the game. The opposing team had the ball.

The television commentator announced with finality that the only thing the opposing team had to do was throw the ball into play and make one successful pass, and the game would be over. That seemed to be a fairly easy feat for players at the professional level.

The announcer hadn't quite factored into his calculations that the players were facing Michael Jordan.

When the ball was thrown in, Jordan seemed to appear out of nowhere and intercepted the inbound pass. He spun around the opposing player, raced down the court, and made a three-point shot just as the buzzer sounded. The Bulls won the game!

Jordan didn't do this only once or twice in his career. He was consistently spectacular, and especially in high-pressure situations. He had an amazing ability to elevate his game just when the circumstances were the most critical.

There have been many outstanding NBA players, but if you ask the knowledgeable man on the street, "Who was the best NBA player at winning games in the final seconds?" the answer would have to be Michael Jordan.

How do people become superstar performers in the face of intense pressure?

I found an answer at a time when I wasn't looking for it.

I was preparing a presentation for a group of top sales performers, who are not the most patient audience members.

If you don't bring new information to them, and present it in a compelling and entertaining way, the smartphones start glowing like the lighters at a rock concert.

As I began to plan for this presentation, I asked myself, *Is there a situation that frequently troubles this group?* I asked several highly successful salesmen the question and sure enough, an answer began to emerge.

These people scored major numbers for their company. They were not short on raw motivation. They really wanted to succeed and have big incentives to do so. But they seemed too often to lose focus and motivation and drift away from pursuing their highest priority work.

"Andy, I know what I should, could, and need to do. But I am just so busy. I just don't have time. I just can't seem to stay focused and motivated." They were suffering from *Why don't I do what I know I should?*

Going over the interview notes I began to wonder if there was a way to generate focus. Is there a way to create a more consistent motivation toward improvement?

I sought out Dr. Habril, a sports psychologist at the United States Olympic Training Center (USOTC). His primary role there is to take new athletes, full of raw motivation and big dreams and goals, and impart to them the mental skills that can turn their motivation into a powerful, lasting force that remains focused until a final gold-medal event.

I asked Dr. Habril, "If you were trying to help a nonathlete, a busy person who wanted to achieve more of their goals, what would you advise that person to do?"

He replied, "Andy, I would teach them the same thing I teach our athletes. Most people are juggling the same categories of responsibilities, whether they are athletes or nonathletes. They are juggling responsibilities to family members, friends, teammates, finances, and ultimately their 'performance' on the job. Most people have high pressure in balancing that. What most people need is a profound but simple shift in their *thinking*.

"They need to shift their focus from outcome—which in my world is winning a gold medal—to focusing exclusively on execution. They need to focus on what it takes to ensure they are in the optimal mental and physical state required to capture every opportunity. It is the process of executing in the moment that is vital. It isn't a focus on two years from now, or four years from now. It is on what needs to be done today to be ready for the moment down the line."

Back to Michael Jordan . . . the announcer had his view of how the game was going to go. But what was Michael Jordan thinking? Before the inbound pass, he was likely thinking, "I am going to win the game."

But as play began, Michael Jordan shifted into *instinct and execution*. His experience gave him instincts. He instinctively responded to the subtle shift in the way the inbound pass was thrown, and anticipated to which player the pass was going to go. He didn't *think* about it. He just instinctively reacted!

As he nears the player, Jordan knows that if he reaches to steal the ball with his inside hand, it shortens his reach by four to six inches. Jordan instinctively executes a perfect outside hand reach, and it is just enough to get a fingertip on the ball. Now the ball is loose and the opposing player is right in front of him. He knows that if he stops in front of or lets his momentum carry him into the opposing player, he will lose his advantage. Jordan instinctively executes a perfect spin move around the opposing player, keeping his momentum moving toward the opposing team's goal. Now he is sprinting down the court, alone.

Put yourself in Jordan's shoes. You are running down the court all alone, millions of people are watching you on television, you look up to find the goal to shoot this long distance three-point shot, and see hundreds of the other team's fans behind the glass backboard. They are trying to distract you by screaming wildly and frantically waving red foam noodles. It is a madhouse of distraction, pressure, and stress. As you finally make it to the three-point line, you hear what sounds like a herd of elephants chasing behind you, which is the opposing team racing to catch you. The clock is ticking down: four, three, two. . . . As you reach the three-point line, you have an amazing opportunity to win, but also loads of pressure. You are alone, in front of everyone.

Are you wondering whether you are going to make the shot and be the hero? Are you worried you might miss and fail miserably? In either case, you likely going to miss.

Thrivers primarily focus on execution, especially when they are under pressure.

Strivers spend a lot of time worrying about possible outcomes.

What Dr. Habril was advocating was essentially, "Practice executing the skills you need to be successful until you don't have to think about them." Stay focused on the practice of execution rather than the final goal or your desired outcome and your mind and body will instinctually react and successfully execute. Hone your execution and if you do so, the skills and mind-sets you need to be successful will be there when you need them.

Barry, a salesman, stays in the execution zone of making calls, setting up appointments, listening closely to what a client needs, and instinctively responding to meet the client's needs. He always has a pen filled with plenty of ink to sign the purchase requisition. His results are more sales, more focus, more motivation, and a much lower daily rate of perceived exertion (RPE). The focus needs to be adjusted to the *skillful execution of successful processes*.

Each person will take one of two mind-sets into a day. The first mind-set is focused on the possible outcomes, or what

might happen in that day. The second mind-set is on executing their best that day.

The more effective mind-set is the second one. And it
is the mind-set that most people don't have. They become
anxious as the hours tick by that they aren't going to reach
their goal.

Those who stay focused on how they are pursuing the
process of their work tend to be more relaxed and find their
stride and stick with it—with far less anxiety—and stay more
positive and flexible in their tone of voice and communication
skills.

They are focused on the way they are playing the business
game, not on the final score they want to see on the board.

Jordan simply broke down winning an almost unwinnable
game, a BHAG to be sure, into three executable skills. Skills
he has mastered though preparation and practice. The skills
answered the following three questions: (1) How do you steal
a ball being inbounded? (2) How do you get around a player
standing in your way? (3) How can you make a three-point
shot under pressure? Those three outcomes were broken
down into specific mini-patterns, which after diligent practice
became second nature to Jordan. Most BHAGs are accomplished with day-to-day persistence, and each day is a series
of mini-patterns.

DOES THE FINISH LINE MATTER?

When I told Janet that she would reach her goals by
"June 31," I wasn't being impish. Well, maybe a little! But
from a larger perspective, I was truly being instructive in
helping her adopt a more successful and less stressful focus—
execution beats outcome seven days a week.

I certainly understand the need for clearly defined outcomes. Finish lines motivate us to run a race, and at the same

time give us a somewhat fixed understanding of our progress and the remaining distance ahead of us. This is only motivating, however, if you truly believe you can make it to the finish line. I wanted Janet to shift her perspective, and shock her a bit into taking a more motivating, day-by-day approach to the changes she already wanted to make.

In many areas of life, there are countless factors that keep a finish line hidden from sight. Nobody knows, if, when, or in what manner life is going to proceed.

That can make a person feel out of control, which is one of, if not the most, demotivating mind-sets you can experience.

Do you remember the first rollercoaster you ever rode? Sometimes you could see the dips and drops, but often it was a surprise. Even if you could see what was going to happen, you didn't feel any less anxiety or dramatic build-up as the rollercoaster ride began.

The more times you rode the rollercoaster, however, the more you learned to anticipate its big dips and turns and the more your anxiety decreased. Even though it was still a stressful situation and you were no more in "control" of the ride than you had been the first time you boarded it, your anxiety was significantly less. You knew when the dips and drops were coming. You were less anxious. You knew when you could relax and when to prepare mentally and lean into the turns. You *felt* more in control.

With the Change Your Day approach, you learn where the dips are in your day, when you can fully relax and when to productively lean into those dips in a productive way.

Expect this same feeling of control to develop as you Change Your Day. You won't be in control of an outcome. But you will be in more control of yourself and *can* have a feeling of control related to the process you have developed— and you can feel in control of your responses to triggers, your mini-patterns, and your attitudes and values.

CONSISTENCY IS WHAT *REALLY* MATTERS

My wife and I finally gave in and got a puppy. We actually got two puppies—a brother and a sister. My children had been asking for a puppy for months. I was the only one in the family who had ever had a puppy, and I was therefore the only one capable of seeing past the fun to the potty training.

Potty training a puppy is a matter of constant vigilance. You have to watch a puppy's every move and scoop it up and get it outside at the first sign of its need to go. There are always false alarms, and there are always missed opportunities!

In life, it is improbable, if not impossible, to stay focused so as to catch all mistakes in advance. You simply have to figure out how to do *better*, without expecting to be perfect. Nobody gets it right every time, all the time.

The goal must become *consistency*. The goal is to set in place a pattern of DOing that becomes habitual, to the degree that life seems to have something "missing" if certain behaviors are forgotten or left undone.

Don't stop too often to evaluate yourself on your progress toward a goal. You'll become too easily frustrated by the fluctuations you see. Frustration with progress at work one day does not mean you are off target. For example, water retention must not be confused with genuine fat gain. A sore muscle must not become a reason to quit. An angry outburst must not be seen as a signal that a relationship is over.

Stay in the flow of the process and evaluate yourself on your own consistency. Are you doing what you have set out to do? Are you doing it as consistently as you can? Are you picking yourself up after a failure and moving forward? Are you forgiving yourself and others so that you don't get stuck in yesterday's news?

If so, you are on the path that *will* lead to success.

To Change Your Day . . .

Remember:

- Settle on a set of patterns and attitudes that you believe will gain you the greatest possible fulfillment and satisfaction. And then stick with those patterns and attitudes. Don't budge from them.

- Don't let your mind wander into future outcomes. Thrivers trust in an execution mind-set. Nobody can predict when, what, or under what conditions the future is going to unfold. The only thing a person truly *can* do is to focus on the processes of today—and live them out to the max. That's not only going to produce personal peace in the present tense, it's going to be the best possible preparation for *whatever* the future holds. *Enjoy* the process and take great joy in the rewards!

CHAPTER 16

Motives and Meaning

Television networks seem to have a particularly strong penchant these days for crime shows. For the most part, I like them! They allow me to think of myself as an amateur detective and I feel great if I can figure out "who done it" before the end of the program. My favorite part of discovering the villain is to decipher their motive. It's important in solving television crimes to know *why* somebody might want to commit a particular crime in order to nail down just *who* committed the crime.

A motive, of course, is something that causes a person to act in a certain way or do a certain thing.

What is *your* motive for getting up tomorrow morning and going to *your* job? Why do you do that particular job when you likely could do a hundred other jobs—even in a lousy economy?

What is your motive for sticking with your present job? What is your motive for putting in the overtime hours and maximum energy?

In the end, your *motive* is directly related to your *motivation*, the ongoing force that compels you to be productive and produce quality work. The quality of your motive is also a strong determinate of your daily rate of perceived exertion (RPE), or how hard it feels to do your work every day.

For many people, a personal motive is not remotely connected to a corporate mission statement. I once was consulting with an organization that helps people with end-of-life care. I asked for a show of hands to the question, "Who can recite this organization's mission statement?" Only one person raised his hand—the CEO!

It was an awkward moment for the CEO, for others in the room, and for me. I quickly rebounded, however, and stated that a corporate mission statement is not nearly as important as an informal "understanding" or definition of the way an organization helps people. I asked, "How many of you can tell your distant relatives at a Thanksgiving dinner table what your organization does to make a difference in at least *some-one's* life?" Every hand went up.

That answer can be a powerful motive for getting up and working hard every day. I continued, "I challenge you to take *that* answer and turn it into your own personal workplace 'mission statement.' Write, 'I work here because this place . . .' Put that statement someplace where you can look at it periodically, and especially on days that seem especially demanding. Why you work where you work and why you choose to do what you do is important. If you have no why, you will find that your enthusiasm is very shallow, your energy is often lower than you would expect, and your motivation walks out the door before you do. Have a why."

A why answer speaks to "meaning." It speaks to purpose. And having meaning and purpose are highly motivating.

"Meaning" does not have to be an in-depth soul-searching exercise done with a guru on the top of a mountain. "Meaning" can simply be a recognition of what you enjoy about your work.

INFUSING MEANING INTO YOUR WORK

It is common sense that most people want more meaning connected to their work and that we would all benefit from it. There is a vast amount of credible research to show that people are better at their work and more committed to their employer if they enjoy what they do, see their work as linked to their personal core values, and feel as if they are part of something bigger than themselves.

I do not agree, however, with the platitude that states, "Love what you do and you'll never work a day in your life."

Work is equated to effort. And those who love what they do generally exert a great deal of effort. Furthermore, love is a very strong emotional word. I greatly enjoy my job. I *work* at it. I love my wife and daughters. Yet, I also love the *moments* at work.

I've had wonderful, emotional, powerful moments when someone phones or e-mails to say that they have made a better life for themselves with the ideas I provided. Or someone on the verge of tears after a presentation saying, "Andy, you don't know how much I needed to hear that today." Or, one of my favorites, "Andy, I would have enjoyed your presentation a lot more if you weren't talking about me the whole time."

I do love those moments. I also really enjoy speaking, collaborating, creating, learning, and so on. But, believe me, most of my workday is work. On the other hand, I do *not* love paperwork, scheduling, staff issues (sorry, Nanci), and trying to convince overly busy people of the value of what I do. Hey, sometimes people are mean.

I know I'm not alone. Author Shane J. Lopez, PhD (*Making Hope Happen*) has surveyed thousands of working adults, only to find that only *1 percent* love their jobs. I am going to translate love here as "enjoying deeply" what they do or "feeling good" about what they do.

Let me assure you that you don't have to enjoy every aspect of your work to be good at it. If you are going to thrive under high demand, however, you must know what about it you do enjoy, feel that your work is connected to your core values, and feel as if you are contributing something that goes beyond your personal needs and ego.

Thrivers generally:

- Can tell you what they enjoy about their work—they can point out the value of their work to them, even if you don't share their values or see their job in the same light that *they* see their job.

- See a connection between their most productive work and their personal values, and they often remind themselves of that connection if frustration or fatigue sets in.
- See their job as being linked to something good, and something important or beneficial.

Work enjoyment can be illustrated as a pyramid (see Figure 16.1), with personal enjoyment as the foundation, a link between enjoyment and values at the next level up the pyramid, and work and positive outcomes beyond self at the top of the pyramid.

Anytime you simplify a big idea, meaning, there are always a few caveats. One, there are some people who already have the "meaning" piece of the Thriving equation figured out. If that is you, thanks for buying this book (just kidding!). Two, some people would put congruence at the top of the pyramid. That's okay by me. This book is not a "follow my all-knowing ideas exactly the same for as every other person on the planet" kind of book. The Meaning Pyramid model is simply a way to clarify values and guide you to get more energy at work by pumping up your sense of meaning and enjoyment at work.

This is more than only my opinion. I'm a research guy. A randomized, placebo-controlled, double-blind kind of research guy. When other experts mention "meaning at work" or especially "purpose," I mentally roll my eyes, expecting that we are headed into the territory of unicorns, pixie dust, and Sasquatch.

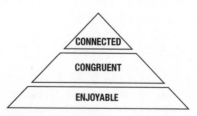

FIGURE 16.1 Meaning Pyramid

Doug Hall, a fantastic thought-leader on the science of innovation and marketing has a saying that sums up my approach: "In God we trust. Everyone else must bring data."

I want to hear what people know, not what they think they know. Or at least tell me what you are reasonably assured works. Sometimes there is just not enough scientific evidence and you have to be philosophical. Luckily, we are not going there.

A 2011 combined study from Portland State and the University of Michigan identified the top breaks that Thrivers use to stay energized at work. The breaks that were connected to increasing vitality and reducing fatigue were:

- Focus on what gives me joy in my work.
- Reflect on how I make a difference at work.
- Reflect on the meaning of my work.

For example, in an interview series created by Mashable and Portal A called "A Day in the Life," Scott Heiferman, CEO of MeetUp, contributed some really interesting and meaningful related statements.

Doing More of What You Enjoy

You can tell in seconds that Scott enjoys his work and takes it very seriously. You can also see that he's identified what he does that creates the best results. "I find time every day to either interact with people in a MeetUp community, or more likely, just looking at what is going on (in the MeetUp communities)."

The Other Meaningful Work

Scott, like most leaders who are ultimately judged by the results they can produce, has evolved how he approaches his work so his time is the most meaningful.

Scott says that he used to have breakfast and dinner meetings, coaching entrepreneurs, etc., but now he has refined the meaningful work for him "to make the best damn product I can, and build the best damn team building the best damn product I can."

And he finishes with, "I'd love to do a bunch of other stuff . . . but that is not my job."

I don't recommend saying, "That is not my job" at work, at least not without some forethought. But you should say it to yourself. A lot.

Thrivers know what is their most productive work and what is a time and brain drain.

To some, this may sound simplistic, to determine what really is your job, the most productive work that you do. If you do know what moves the needle most for you at work, then take a breath and soak in the fact that most don't and that you are way down the road to successful work and less stress. But most people don't. If you don't know or are not doing what is most important most of the time, then you could be SO much more productive and accomplished and less stressed by intentionally combining a growing understanding of what it really is that moves the needle at work with some thought around what you really enjoy.

A PERSONAL EVALUATION

Let me be quick to add that enjoyment, satisfaction, and contribution are not traits that are universally objective. In other words, what *you* find enjoyable, fulfilling, or meaningful may not be what I personally find enjoyable, fulfilling, or meaningful. You should be able to isolate what leads you to define your own job in those terms, or recognize that your job is *not* associated with those traits. My point is this: You need to evaluate your own job when it comes to the happiness, worth, or satisfaction it gives you. What works for you is what you will work at best, hardest, and longest. And that's your choice according to your definitions!

I encourage you to

- Focus on what gives you the greatest joy and meaning at work—be able to define it.
- Reflect on how you are making a difference at work and through your work—be able to give examples.
- Reflect on the meaning of your work as it relates to your core values.
- And then . . . seek to increase what you enjoy!

The more you burrow into what holds greatest meaning, fulfillment, and greatest happiness in your job, the more you are going to be in better focus as a whole person, and the more you will be able to cope with aspects of your job that may not be always be as fulfilling or rewarding as you would like them to be. You can come to find that the "administrivia," the mundane and routine chores required of you, and the not-so-exciting aspects of your work become easier to do, and get completed more quickly, if you have a strong focus on what you DO find exciting, rewarding, or fulfilling. Working within the core of your own joy at work will enable you to have more overall energy and momentum, which makes doing the tedious chores less worthy of complaint or stress.

The Thriver Zone is generally the overlap of what you enjoy doing and what you do most productively (see Figure 16.2). Enjoyment is directly linked to productivity—a person does more and does it better if the "doing" is more enjoyable.

I'm not suggesting that you should be able to spend all your time in the Thriver Zone, but I have found that Thrivers spend more time in this Zone than Strivers. There is a lot of enjoyment that comes from accomplishment—both knowing what works, and knowing that you are doing what works. Find

FIGURE 16.2 The Thriver Zone

your Thriver Zone at work, be clear enough on it that you have it on the tip of your tongue and at the top of your mind, and you have the makings for more energy and reaching high altitudes of happiness at work.

But don't stop there. Dig deeper than just what you enjoy. Scott says that it's important to "scrutinize your calendar and determine whether how you are spending your time is true to what you are trying to do in the world."

He recommends, "Take a breath and soak in what is going on right now. It's really easy to get wrapped up in your own head or in the money side of things. It is so important to stay connected to what we are really trying to do."

He says, "If I'm having a bad day, all I have to do is think about the fact that people whom I care about are going to benefit from a MeetUp at some point.

"That is part of a larger change in the world, that MeetUp is one part of, which is people turning to each other. That is where the world is going and we are helping to bring on that change."

These simple thoughts adapted to your work can help you feel congruent and connected. It is easy to see that Scott's core values include making a better world through giving people opportunities in "turning to each other," to "meet up."

He obviously feels at his best when he is helping others and doing what is important to him; specifically, he believes that a better world is made by people turning to each other and that he, his teams, company, volunteers, and MeetUp community are helping make that happen.

I've never gone into a company or team of people and thought, "You know, this organization spends way too much time helping their people understand why they are work-ing so hard and how their work benefits others outside of this organization." But I have thought many times that the people in this company are just working for a paycheck, and that they could increase employee loyalty, engagement, and bottom-line results if they would help them understand in a nonbland, mission-statement sort of way how their work both drives the financial success of their organization and how it is connected to the good of their communities and their people.

Trigger: Feeling frustrated or overwhelmed.
Pattern: "What is this all about anyway?"

MEANING IS MOTIVATING, EVEN AT UNSEEN LEVELS

I once consulted with a company that manages roadways. They paint lines on the roads, manage toll booths, spray weeds at the side of the roads and public waterways, and so forth. One day I was giving a presentation to a group about the value of what they did, and how they made life better in the community. I was near the height of my inspirational message when one man piped up, "Andy, I spray weeds. Don't get carried away. It's a job."

I hit pause on all my thoughts about safe, beautiful trans-portation and ecological benefits for the roads and waterways and asked this man, "So, why do you do what you do? Why do you do *this* job?" He replied with what I considered to be a great slogan for this entire division. He said, "I keep Florida Florida." I could have boiled my entire presentation down to those four words.

Floridians *want* a state with beautiful and safe highways and clear and ecologically healthy waterways. I encouraged all the people in that room to take on this man's perspective. What they were doing was beautifying and protecting the "value" of their home state—value as a place to live and value as a tourist destination. Now *that* was connecting their work to a purpose that was meaningful and beyond their own paycheck.

Meaning in Service

Not long ago a supervisor was making her rounds around her company. She came upon a man fixing a piece of equipment and asked, "Do you enjoy what you do?" The man grinned. His work was tedious. People only called upon him when they were highly stressed or frustrated. He said, "I do like my job."

"What do you like about it?" she asked, genuinely interested in what he might say.

"Well, I know my paycheck is going to feed my wife and me, and put a roof over our heads. At work, as I am repairing a machine, many people begin with sharing their frustrations with me, but we end up sharing what is good in their work, their life. I know that I have three interns, at present, who come to me after work to hang out and talk. I suspect that I might be the most influential male figure in their lives. That's something that is important to me." The supervisor related this to me: "This man had a better take on his job than I had at that point. I knew I valued my salary, but I couldn't point to individual people I was helping, at least not in a way that I *knew* I was helping them or that they were grateful for my help. And, I took work home every night and asked my husband and two children to accommodate mommy's need to do *her* homework rather than helping them with their homework. This man caused me to take a new look at my life and make some serious adjustments!"

There Is a Better Way to Start Your Day

I had the opportunity to interview one of the leading sport psychologists in the United States. I was asking questions around the idea "What mental skills can you share with hard-working adults that you've seen work in hard-working athletes?" He mentioned that one of the most beneficial exercises he does with his athletes is helping them define their "First Thought."

"What is your first thought after your alarm clock rings you into consciousness?" I've asked people all over the world. The answers are pretty common.

"I need to pee." Not the most motivational thought, but functional.

"Ugh, where is the snooze button." Nothing like starting the day with a little procrastination.

"It seems like I just did this!" Another day? Is that good news or bad?

"I've got so much to do today, I've got to get up." It's normal to default to this thought process. But is it the best angle?

Of these examples, did you notice any that would motivate a great day? Set the tone, ring the bell in a way that energizes and focuses you in the right direction?

Remember the Core Concept that Motivation is simply Momentum in Disguise.

My psychologist friend would have you not only define your "Meaning Statement" but use it as your first thought.

If you had the chance to sit down with him, he would ask you, "Why are you sacrificing so much?" He would then take your well-thought-out answer and say, "So that you can what?" Then you would respond and he would repeat that soon-to-be-annoying question, "So that you can what?" and keep repeating it until you came upon a thought that you could repeat that summarized why you are working so hard and felt comfortable saying it (at least to yourself).

Then, once that thought is solidified, he would instruct you to not only make this your first thought, but you are to smile as you say it because the bio-feedback of smiling has been shown to improve attitude.

I tried this suggestion the very next day. I woke, repeated my thought in my mind, and smiled. My wife looked over at me and said, "Forget about it."

To Change Your Day . . .

- I challenge you right now to list five things you enjoy about your work. You may want to do this in a small-group setting, challenging one another around a break table to list the top five factors about your jobs that give you pleasure or fulfillment. Then compare your lists! Talk about what you value at your place of employment. Talk about how you might make things *more* enjoyable.

- I challenge you to name three ways in which what you do serves your core values. In what ways are your work and your daily activities aligning with what you believe in personally?

- I challenge you to think of one way in which your work and coworkers and/or clients are serving a unified greater purpose? How are you making your community or the world in general better?

CHAPTER 17

The Power of Attitude

Much can and has been said about attitude, and most people believe that attitude is not only important to personal success but a powerful influencer in relationships of all types. What I want to challenge you to do today is to evaluate your attitude according to one main criterion: well-being.

In 2007–2008 Towers Perrin published its Global Workforce Study, which was a very large poll of 90,000 respondents in 18 nations. The study concluded that the number-one driver of employee engagement was this: "Senior management's sincere interest in employee well-being."

We've long known that "people don't care about what you know until they know you care." This study affirmed, however, that most workers want their employers or supervisors to care about them, and in a way that recognizes the whole of their humanity, not only the quality of the tasks they perform for a company. And that is what truly makes them want to give their best for the company, more so than even pay.

A key question to ask yourself is this: How do I sincerely display that I am concerned about the well-being of the people around me? This question applies to all areas of work and life. How do you *show* you care?

One of the foremost ways is by being predictable in the expression of your own values, and by affording others around you a sense that they are secure in their relationship with you and that you value them. Another way is to help others establish patterns with you that support your relationship.

I often ask my clients to write out a list of people who are important to them:

- Family members
- Friends
- Mentors

- Coworkers who are "team members"
- People who have sacrificed to help you
- . . . And so forth.

And then to identify people by name in the various categories they've listed.

And then to write next to each person's name: How I show this person I care about their well-being.

This exercise not only helps raise a person's awareness of well-being and of expressing care for others, but the list can help serve as a trigger to give more sincere compliments and words of appreciation, and to put in place a more regular series of encounters (by phone, note, or face-to-face meeting over lunch or coffee) to bolster or renew relationships.

Showing you sincerely care about the well-being, including the security, of those at work and in your personal life is an important and clear way to Change Your Day and energize others as well as yourself.

ARE YOU HOPEFUL?

A second question about your attitude: Are you hopeful? Are you generally optimistic about both the present and the future?

Dan Burrus, a technology futurist, has said, "Your view of the future shapes your actions today, and your actions today shape your future." My questions to many of my clients are: "Do you believe tomorrow can be better than today—and that five years from now, your life will be very much better than now? Do you believe things *can* and *will* improve?"

If you see the future in dark and ominous terms, your immediate tomorrow is likely to be a rather horrible abyss.

On the other hand, if you refuse to give in to doom-and-gloom forecasts, negative predictions, and dire speculations, then you are likely to get through both today and tomorrow with a brighter outlook and more life-improving accomplishments.

Do you have a deep feeling of confidence?

A focus on well-being . . . a hopeful and optimistic outlook . . . can sink deep into a person to create abiding confidence.

In addition, confidence is rooted in a person's self-awareness that he has knowledge and skills that are valuable. Knowledge is information—including understanding how bits and pieces of information work together. Skills are abilities that can be learned, practiced, and developed to a state in which the *doing* of the skill is almost automatic. Skills are behavioral. Knowledge is mental. Confidence requires both.

The Big Three Enemies of Confidence. Do your utmost to guard your confidence and to avoid the foremost enemies of confidence.

In my opinion, there are three major enemies of confidence, and every person is wise to know what they are to avoid them. None of these enemies, by the way, is rooted in self-esteem. A person can have very high self-esteem—related to his value to his family and people he admires, respects, or loves—and still not be confident in a workplace, especially if he is a new hire or if a particular field has changed faster than he has been able to keep up with it.

The three true enemies of confidence are:

1. Perfectionism. A perfectionist will insist that everything is performed correctly or at a hundred-percent level before he or she will take on a task. Creating consistent, positive momentum is a more productive mindset than perfectionism.

2. Pessimism. Pessimists know that perfection is not possible, and they often let this viewpoint discourage them from trying or giving their full efforts to progress. With pessimism as your reaction to challenges, it is easy to constantly battle dark, negative thoughts, especially ones of failure or of being blamed for a failure.
3. Procrastination. Out of a perspective of pessimism, a person often delays "trying." Since he sees no value in completion that doesn't include top-mark perfection, he puts off doing anything.

All three of these enemies of confidence are descriptive of a person with one foot on the accelerator and the other on the brake. Work performance is herky-jerky, with very little forward progress and a growing loss of motivation and energy.

Confidence is maintained by taking the 180-degree opposite approach: take charge of your attitude and choose to be someone who does his best to be excellent but who is also committed to being a "completionist" (a person who gets a job done) . . . by staying optimistic . . . by having the belief that if you execute, the results will come . . . and by refusing to put off until tomorrow what you know can and should be done today.

FORGIVE YESTERDAY AND WORK ON TODAY

It was a slate-gray Friday afternoon in Bentonville, Arkansas. I was sitting at a U-shaped table with 18 high-performance, high-stress people from the Gillette Company. This was our third monthly meeting. My role was to help them learn to "stress right," which means to adopt the thought processes and daily patterns that work best in times of intense work demands.

The agenda was in place. We would recap how each person did individually during the previous month, and then I'd present new goals and teach additional techniques for the coming month. The immediate goal they had been working on was actively focusing on the positive potential in their day, rather than seeing potential for disaster.

The program was designed to encourage workers to focus on practical ways of achieving goals. It calls upon a person to focus more on what they have accomplished, and less on where they fell short of the ideal. To essentially see the "one in seven," the one who changes and sustains the changes, in their own day.

I began the meeting with a few quick remarks and then said, "Okay, Sarah, let's start with you." If you met Sarah you would consider her an optimistic if not a bubbly person. She seemed to rush through one instance where she was doing well on the way to reveling in three examples of where she fell short. I paused the meeting and reminded everyone of the goal of the previous month and suggested that they begin with examples of where they were successful in seeing the "one in seven" in themselves over the past month. Without fail, each person would rush through one positive example to give three or four areas where they tripped up.

Sarah reported she continually thought about all the work she still had to do, the deadlines that were looming, falling behind, and feelings of potential failure. I learned something important during that meeting. Successful, hard-working, normally upbeat and optimistic people are often hard on themselves to an unproductive level. They are usually their own worst critics. They needed better bounce-back skills so they could spend more time in a productive state.

My solution is this: Thrivers forgive themselves faster.

Core Concept: Thrivers forgive themselves faster.

Not always, but very often, I find that Strivers are much quicker to forgive others their faults and failures—especially in the normal flow of work life—than they are to forgive themselves.

I am *not* saying that we should be wantonly self-indulgent or set low standards for ourselves. I am saying that we need to take responsibility for our mistakes, apologize when appropriate, make amends as necessary, and then "let it go." Forgiveness is not exoneration, saying that there are no consequences. Neither is forgiveness a statement that something didn't happen, didn't matter, or shouldn't be addressed. Forgiveness is refusing to linger on the bad thing that happened, either by commission or omission. It is addressing the fault or failure and then refusing to allow it to inhibit future action. Forgiveness is "letting go" of all guilt, condemnation, or pessimism that can occur after a failure.

Treat yourself with the compassion and generosity you'd extend to another person who had made a mistake or fallen short of an ideal or goal. Put yourself on a path of personal encouragement toward a brighter tomorrow.

Forgive yesterday—let it go. And work on today.

One of my past coaches had a two-hour rule. If you had a bad performance, then you had two hours. You could pout, scream, cry, crawl into cave and isolate yourself, or do whatever you think will help you deal with the disappointment. But when the two hours post event are up, no more. It is time to start moving forward again.

In a weight-loss study of people who had trouble with binge eating, researchers found that just one day of "self-compassion" training tripled their long-term success.

In another study involving dieting willpower, researchers found that self-compassion improved willpower to make smart choices, and reduced the urge for emotional eating.

Forgive yourself fast. Be compassionate to yourself. You'll recover from a failure faster and more fully. Forgiveness has been correlated with a wide range of benefits—including lower blood pressure, a stronger immune system, a reduction of stress hormones in the blood, fewer stomach problems, less back pain, fewer and less severe headaches . . . and more. The list of benefits is very long!

If there's someone you need to forgive today, do so.

If you need to forgive yourself, now is the moment!

KEEP ON KEEPING ON

But, you may be asking, what about a work or home environment that is not all that great—perhaps one that is downright painful or difficult. Isn't having an upbeat attitude hypocritical or "fake"?

Not necessarily.

One day I was at a local fitness center and I asked a man named Bob how he felt after a rigorous cycling class, which just happened to have been held on the second of January—a time when New Year's resolutions kick in. He looked at me with a "get away from me, weirdo" look. He was in pain and exhaustion and there was nothing good about the experience from his perspective in that moment.

When I asked a local cyclist how she felt after the class, she said, "Andy, it hurt so good!"

Attitude made the difference. Sarah saw benefit in her pain and exhaustion. Bob didn't, at least not yet.

There's nothing at all hypocritical about being positive in a negative situation. There's only hypocrisy in voicing positive words about a negative environment if you truly feel negative.

A positive word and a positive attitude in a negative world can make a difference for the good—both of the person with the attitude and of others who witness a positive attitude turned into positive action.

The good news is that Bob came back two days later. The class was still difficult for him. But the more he attended over the ensuing weeks, the more he began to enjoy the exercise. To date, I've now seen Bob in that same class for over two years and not only has he transformed his body, he has also learned to positively embrace the difficulty and the challenge in a motivating way.

That is often true for many people who have a hard time at the outset of facing a change. The challenge is to keep *doing*, and not give up.

Strivers very often have a mind-set of "getting through it."

Thrivers have a mind-set of "getting into it."

If you can make that mental adjustment, you are likely going to want to continue and persevere until the desired change becomes ingrained.

To Change Your Day . . .

Remember:

- Your pursuit of excellence and your enduring in the patterns and attitudes that lead to success is predicated on values related to well-being, genuine hope, execution, and forgiveness.

- Explore more of the "inner you." Choose to create an attitude that becomes the atmosphere in which you live and work.

- Attitude is not something to be put off or put on. It is something that becomes the glue that binds all of your best efforts together. It is the very core of your integrity, and your ability to integrate work and life.

Nothing impacts your day, or the degree to which you can change your day, as much as your attitudes about your day, and about all of your life.

CHAPTER 18

From a Change Underdog to a Challenge Winner

One of my favorite "change underdogs" is Lou. A change underdog is someone who never thought he or she *could* change, but who wanted to change and actually succeeded at change.

Lou was part of a well-being program I conducted for a group of salespeople. There were 36 people in the program, and the only one who was not fully on board was Lou. He would often tease people for making healthier choices, and he was the only person who didn't keep up their "challenge log" for the first month.

The way the program worked was that each month the participants would have a checklist and keep track of how well they did in five very simple categories. They were challenged to:

1. Drink two bottles of water a day (or the equivalent of 32 ounces).
2. Eat two fist-sized servings each of fruit and veggies a day.
3. Eat a snack at 3 o'clock in the afternoon.
4. Lay out their exercise clothes each night, for use the following morning.
5. Accumulate 30 minutes of any form of physical activity each day.

If a person did this, he or she got to check a big yes box for the day. And if not, they had to check the no box. At the end of the month, the boxes were totaled for each person. Twenty boxes (five workdays for four weeks) made for a possible 20 yes marks. At the end of the first month, everyone had checked yes at least 18 of the 20 days.

Except Lou.

Lou didn't turn in a log, and the result was that his score was zero.

What Lou hadn't remembered was that anyone who marked less than 15 of the 20 possible yes boxes received a red X on their log and also on their office door. I had made big red acrylic Xs with an "S" in the middle that stood for Slacker.

Lou had signed the contract with all of the other participants so he could not take the X off his office door until the following monthly meeting.

The X was a real trigger for Lou! It didn't take too many encounters with fellow employees saying, "Hey, what's up, Slacker?" for Lou to get with the program.

Over the next several months, Lou did not miss checking a single yes box. In fact, in a surprisingly short period of time he was beginning to feel so much better that he began to be just a little obnoxious in telling others how much he was *enjoying* the process. He was feeling more energy, had a calmer demeanor, and was able to focus better. Momentum was building for Lou. He ended up building momentum throughout the rest of the "challenge," and along the way, he lost a significant amount of weight, updated his wardrobe to reveal the new "Lean Lou," and scored high on all measures of health.

Lou not only won the challenge the first year, but every year for the next four years!

If Lou was sitting next to you right now, he would be quick to tell you that not only did he experience better health and more stress relief, but he became a better salesman, coworker, and generally a better *person*.

Go back and read the five things in the challenge. They were simple changes that cost virtually nothing and didn't take a great deal of time. They were doable. And most important of all, they were required on a *daily* basis.

My point is this: If *Lou* could be a change underdog who went on to be a challenge winner, you can be one, too!

AND THEN THERE'S MOM . . .

Have you ever tried to tell your mother what to do? My mother, Jacquie, was 49 when she began a "change your day" program.

Mom has bright blue eyes and a soft voice, but not long *before* starting her program, she had quit smoking. It hadn't been easy. She had smoked heavily for 31 years, and over the six months after she quit smoking she gained 40 pounds. Her beautiful eyes seemed to recede into her face and her voice had a hard edge to it. Others may not have noticed, but I am, after all, her *son*.

One afternoon I blurted out to her before I could stop myself, "Mom, you have *got* to lose weight." She didn't say a word. I was given the silent treatment.

The next day, however, Mom called and, with resignation in her voice, she asked, "Well, what should I do?" I started her on a simple walking plan—five 30-minute walks a week.

Nearly every night for three consecutive weeks she called me to say, "I don't think I can do this. Walking makes me tired. I don't have time for it. It's not working because I still weigh the same."

I said, admittedly without much compassion, "Mom, you're being a baby. Just keep walking."

One evening there was no call. Had something gone wrong? I called her. "Mom, I'm worried you didn't make it back from your walk."

She said, "Andy, I'm a big girl and according to you, too big a girl. My walking is fine. It's just part of my day now. It's nothing worth reporting." It was a moment of celebration for me. I knew my mother's new daily routine had built real momentum toward a new good habit!

Three weeks later, she called to say, "During my usual walk a woman about my age and size jogged past me. Do you think I could jog?"

I said, "Mom, you don't need to run."

She replied, "I know I don't *need* to run. I want to run."

The next day she started on a program to become a 30-minute runner over the next 30 days. Each week she got stronger and more confident. There were days she called with uncertainty about her next day's goal. I encouraged her to keep her pace slow and her mind positive.

The day before her first 30-minute run (at the end of the 30 days), she was very nervous. I reminded her that she had already succeeded.

The next day she called and I could almost hear her jumping up and down. "Andy, it worked! I ran 30 minutes nonstop. I am a runner." I started jumping up and down, too. Three weeks later, she participated in a Race for the Cure, a 5k run. She completed the 3.1-mile race nonstop and after it was over, she said, "I cannot believe it was so easy. This is one of the best things I have ever done."

That was then. My mother completed 10 full 26.2-mile marathons. She ran the Pikes Peak Marathon, the Great Wall of China Marathon, has qualified for and run the Boston Marathon five times, and, six years ago, she completed the Lake Placid Ironman Triathlon, which consisted of 2.4 miles of lake swimming, 110 miles of biking through the Adirondack Mountains, and then a full marathon. That was 15 hours of constant exercise, all at the age of 53.

Mom didn't start out believing she could be an exerciser. It had never dawned on her to become a runner. It would have been unthinkable to her initially to even consider participating in an event like a triathlon. Her simple beginnings with a daily walk ended up building a life for her that was healthier and more vibrant than she had ever experienced.

Along with her newfound physical vitality, she had more confidence, greater mental clarity, and more energy to pour into her work. She was promoted at her workplace, a hospital. The marketing department saw such fantastic changes in her that they presented her as a role model of the type of employee they wanted to represent the hospital to the community. They put her photograph and a description of her on a large billboard positioned next to one of the most heavily traveled roads in her city! She's not just a role model, she's a *famous* role model!

Way to go, Mom.

She was the kind of person who would shrink away from compliments, much less accolades. What she did, she did for herself and for her family. What Mom did in changing her day to include a 30-minute walk changed the way her family and coworkers thought of her, and the way she thought of herself. Her daily change ended up changing the quality of her *entire* life. Remember that she didn't set out to change her *life*. She simply set out to change her *day*. And then, by changing her day, she changed her life.

MORE AND MORE GREAT DAYS

Both Lou and my mother discovered that the best part of changing a day means that a person is likely to experience more and more great days, and fewer and fewer bad days.

I strongly encourage you to make it your goal to have more and more great days. Not every day can be stellar. Life happens. You get told "no," the car breaks down, the unexpected bill shows up in the mail, the bad news comes from afar. BUT . . . if you are executing what you personally define as the basics for a great day, you CAN have more and more great days. Make that your perspective and your goal.

Ultimately, all of life is a series of days. Goals that are scheduled to be annual, quarterly, monthly, or even weekly achievements are necessary and beneficial. In one sense, you *know* that time is broken down into weeks, months, and years. In most cases, however, you likely have learned that long-range goals are nearly always reached by meeting *daily* quotas or *daily* goals. In fact, many businesses have found that they can predict by the 10th of any given month if the business is going to make its monthly goal, and by the end of one month if a quarterly goal is going to be reached.

How UN-motivating is it to continue to pursue a level of performance that you *know* you aren't going to reach? In case you have any doubts, the answer is, not very motivating at all!

On the other hand, it is extremely motivating to set and reach daily goals. If for some reason a daily goal isn't met . . . well, tomorrow, you don't have to change yesterday, only today. If a daily goal is met, you have momentum on your side!

Live in the day.

Change what you don't like—in a day.

Establish new patterns that enhance today.

It will be more than enough.

About the Author

Andy Core is an award-winning lecturer, author, television host, and expert in human performance and motivation. Recently voted a 2012 Top 5 Global Health/Healthcare Speaker by Speakers Platform, Andy has a master's degree in the science of human performance and has spent the past 23 years mastering what it takes to become energized, healthy, motivated, and better equipped to thrive in today's hectic society.

Andy travels throughout the United States, Asia, and Europe working with organizations who are dedicated to increasing the effectiveness of their people by improving their overall well-being.

He lives in Fayetteville, Arkansas, with his wife, Naomi, and their two children, Bella and Camille.

Change Your Day Resources

Go to www.AndyCore.com/resources

CHANGE YOUR DAY VIDEO COURSE

In this online video course, Andy will walk you through how to Change Your Day so that you create sustained motivation, energy, and the ability to accomplish more.

THE THRIVER QUIZ

Is your daily life positioning you to be a Thriver or a Struggler? How effectively are you satisfying the Core Four, which are vital for sustaining a thriving way of life in a high-demand job or work culture. Take this assessment and receive your results immediately by e-mail.

ANDY CORE'S NEWSLETTER

Subscribe to Andy's e-mail newsletter to:

- Learn about new research, how-tos, product reviews, and exclusive interviews that will help you Change Your Day.
- Learn about updated Change Your Day information and new tools.
- Get access and discounts for upcoming books, webinars, and new learning tools.

CUSTOMIZED CONTENT

Andy will study your people and custom design content to help you motivate and equip them to thrive in a high-demand world.

- Live and virtual presentations
- Interviews and articles for your organization's magazine and newsletters
- Branded information you can share with your customers

Index

Note: Page references in *italics* refer to figures.